Hope When Believers Struggle

Studies in Mark's Gospel

Written by

D.L. LOWRIE

Adult January Bible Study 2005

LifeWay Press®

Nashville, TN

ISBN: 0-6330-9669-5

This book is a resource in the Leadership and Skill Development category
of the Christian Growth Study Plan.
Course CG-1041

Subject Area: Bible Studies
Dewey Decimal Classification Number: 226.3
Subject Heading: BIBLE. N.T. MARK—STUDY \ DISCIPLESHIP

Printed in the United States of America

Leadership and Adult Publishing
LifeWay Church Resources
One LifeWay Plaza
Nashville, TN 37234-0175

We believe the Bible has God for its author; salvation for its end; and truth, without any mixture of error, for its matter and that all Scripture is totally true and trustworthy. The 2000 statement of *The Baptist Faith and Message* is our doctrinal guideline.

Cover Image: Corbis

Hope

When Believers Struggle

Studies in Mark's Gospel

From the Editor

Mark's Gospel is the shortest of the four and emphasizes Jesus' actions as proof of His messiahship and deity. Mark also gives special attention to the first people who followed Jesus and His expectations of them. Mark indicates that Jesus' disciples often struggled in their relationship with Jesus, particularly in understanding who He was and in knowing and doing what He expected from them. This study will help adults understand Jesus better, and they will be challenged to live in ways that express a high level of Christian commitment. This study will also help adults identify positive examples of discipleship for believers to appropriate and negative examples for them to avoid.

This Learner Guide for January Bible Study 2005 is designed to help adults understand Mark's Gospel. It is written in an informal, easy-to-read style and explains the biblical text without extensive comments. This Learner Guide has a series of helps to enhance each adult's study. These helps include:

- Two learning activities in each chapter. Each activity is integral to the teaching plans found in the Leader Guide.
- Sets of questions (see "For Your Consideration") found throughout each chapter. The questions can be used in individual or group study. The questions can help an adult probe further after reading the Scripture and related textbook material. Both the questions and the learning activities can help a leader generate discussion.
- At least one feature entitled "A Closer Look" per chapter, which elaborates on or provides summary information on related chapter topics.

Leaders will find further commentary, plans for teaching this study, and teaching-learning items in the *January Bible Study 2005 Expository Notes and Leader Helps* (Adult Leader Guide, ISBN 0-6330-9669-5).

Dr. D. L. Lowrie wrote this issue of January Bible Study. Dr. Lowrie is a retired Southern Baptist pastor living in Lubbock, Texas, He is a member of First Baptist Church in Lubbock.

Stephen W. Carlson, Editor

Session 1

Who Is in Control?

Scripture **Mark 1:1–3:6**
Focal: Mark 1:1-3,9-20,35-39; 2:14-17

When they left China to come to the United States to do research as scientists, they adopted American names—John and Cathy. They were convinced atheists.

The first time John opened a Bible that Cathy had been given, John read these words: "In the beginning God created the heavens and the earth" (Gen. 1:1). John then promptly closed the Bible. He knew that this first verse of the Bible was false, so he assumed the rest of it was false. His study of science had given him a satisfactory explanation for the existence of the universe without God.

A Chinese church near the campus reached out to them, and they began to attend a weekly fellowship and Bible study in the home of retired missionaries. A good meal was included. Other Christians gave them some gifts and witnessed to them. They also prayed for this couple. Their love prompted John and Cathy to open their Bible for a second look.

Soon they became convinced that God did create the universe and that Jesus is the Son of God. This prompted them to become followers of Jesus and to receive Christian baptism. Seeing God as Creator and Jesus as His Son changed their worldview radically. Because of their new faith, they shared the conviction of Jesus' first followers—Jesus is the Son of God and thus He is the One with the right to be in control of their lives.

Mark wrote his Gospel so people would believe that Jesus of Nazareth is the Son of God. It was written so people would decide to become followers of Jesus. Here we meet His first followers (or disciples) and discover how they became convinced that He is the One in control.

NOTE JESUS' INTRODUCTION (MARK 1:1-3)

Mark's Gospel opens with these words: "The beginning of the gospel of Jesus Christ, the Son of God." The Greek word for *gospel* means "good news" and refers to the message about Jesus as Savior.

For Your Consideration

1. What does the title "Christ" tell us about Jesus?

2. What does the title "Son of God" mean when used of Jesus?

3. What does the name Jesus tell us about His mission?

4. Which two prophets foretold the ministry of John the Baptist?

5. What was the primary mission of John the Baptist?

The first verse in Mark's Gospel contains only 12 words but introduces us to the One in charge—Jesus of Nazareth.

The good news is this: Jesus is the Christ, or Messiah. The title "Christ" became almost a personal name for Jesus in the New Testament, for it means "the anointed one." God had promised to send a deliverer to save His people from their sins, and Jesus is the One. He was anointed with the Spirit as were many leaders in the Old Testament. The name "Jesus" calls attention to this mission, for it means "the Lord saves."

Jesus is also the "Son of God." He enjoys a unique and eternal relationship with the Heavenly Father. While His followers come to God as their Father and enjoy a wonderful relationship with Him, Jesus is uniquely the "Son of God." This is good news indeed! The Son of God came to earth.

Isaiah and Malachi joined voices to promise the coming of the Messiah (Mal. 3:1; Isa. 40:3). Mark quoted their promise that a

your notes

A CLOSER LOOK

Sons of God

The Bible refers to several people as sons of God, but the nature of that sonship is not always the same. Here are the main ones:

Angels—by creation (Job 1:6)
Israel—by election (Hos. 11:1; Ex. 4:22-23)
Believers—by regeneration and adoption (1 John 5:1-2; Rom. 8:14,19; Gal. 3:26)
Jesus Christ—by a unique and eternal relationship with the Father (John 3:16,18,35-36; 5:19-27)

special messenger would precede the Messiah to prepare the way (Mark 1:2-3):

> Look, I am sending My messenger ahead of You,
> who will prepare Your way.
> A voice of one crying out in the wilderness:
> "Prepare the way for the Lord;
> make His paths straight!"

This is what John the Baptist did! He introduced the Israelites to their Messiah. He prepared a remnant to receive Him by baptizing them in the waters of the Jordan as a sign of their repentance.

Both prophets indicated that the coming Messiah would be the King. Before a reigning king would visit a province in his kingdom, a herald would precede him, calling on the people to make ready for the visit of the king. As such a herald, John boldly announced to Israel the coming of the King. This is what we need to know—the King of Israel, the Son of God, has come. The promise of the prophets has been fulfilled.

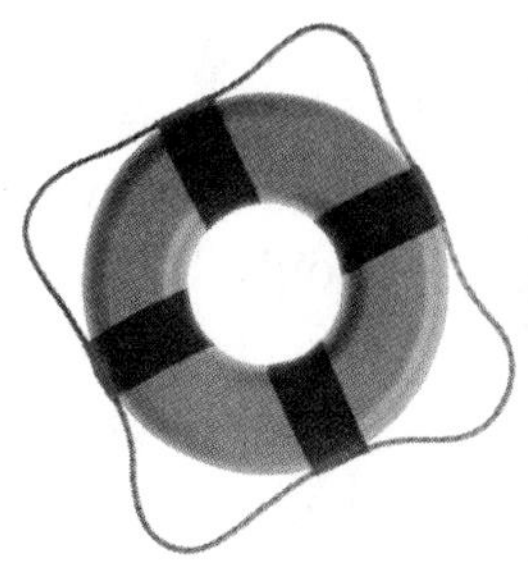

Consider His Divine Approval (Mark 1:9-15)

Even though Jesus was sinless, His baptism by John identified Him with the kingdom of God and with those who were confessing their sins. Jesus traveled from Nazareth to the Jordan to be baptized like the others. During His baptism Jesus received divine approval through a vision and a voice.

For Your Consideration

1. What did Jesus see at His baptism?

2. How was the Holy Spirit like a dove?

3. Why could the Holy Spirit come to rest on Jesus?

4. The words of the Father about Jesus can be found in what Old Testament passages?

5. What followed the vision and the voice?

6. Why did the Father choose this moment to speak?

In the vision, "He saw the heavens being torn open" (Mark 1:10). The skies above the Jordan were suddenly ripped apart by a supernatural force. Then the Holy Spirit—in a fashion reminiscent of the majestic flight of a dove—descended on Jesus. This same Spirit had hovered over the original creation (see Gen. 1:2), but He now rested on Christ. Jesus is the only person on whom the Spirit could fully rest. The Spirit was upon Jesus to empower Him for the mission His Father had assigned.

PhotoDisc

After the descent of the Spirit, the Father's voice sounded from heaven and said: "You are My beloved Son; In You I take delight!" The Father used the words of the psalmist and Isaiah the prophet (Ps. 2:7; Isa. 42:1). As Jesus began His ministry, the Father identified Him as His beloved Son and expressed pleasure with what He was doing. Jesus is the only Person to ever receive such an expression of approval from the Heavenly Father.

This experience was followed by a time of testing in the wilderness (Mark 1:12-13). Satan tempted Jesus to sin during His 40 days in the wilderness, but Jesus thwarted Satan's attempts to destroy His mission just as it was getting started (see Matt. 4:1-11). Then Jesus began sharing the good news of the kingdom of God (Mark 1:14-15). The kingdom of God refers to God's reign on earth in the hearts and lives of individuals. Jesus inaugurated the kingdom and called people to repentance so they can enter the kingdom and live as kingdom citizens. The church is not the same as the kingdom but is part of the kingdom. The purpose of the church is to advance God's kingdom and bring in more kingdom citizens by faith in Jesus. The kingdom will be consummated at Christ's return when God's will is done on earth absolutely as it is now in heaven (see Matt. 6:10).

Respond to His Call (Mark 1:16-20)

Jesus preached and taught as One with authority. Two fishermen, Andrew and Peter, recognized this when Jesus called them to be His disciples.

For your consideration

1. How did Jesus use the word "follow" in verse 17?

2. Why do you think Jesus called two fishermen as His first disciples?

your notes

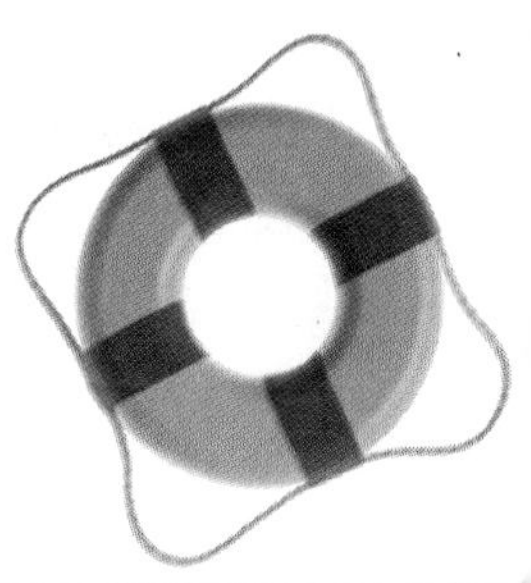

3. What were you doing when Jesus called you to salvation?

4. What promise did Jesus make to those who follow Him?

5. What has following Jesus meant to you?

Learning Activity

Does Jesus Have Control of My Life?

Study the following passages of Scripture. Ask yourself: What do these passages say about Jesus and His control over the lives of people? Write down your reflections about the people who encountered Jesus then, and write down how those experiences apply to people now.

Passage	Then	Now
Mark 1:9-11		
Mark 1:12-13		
Mark 1:14-15		

The brothers Andrew and Peter were involved in their fishing business when Jesus called them. He was very direct—"Follow me." To respond to the command is to acknowledge the authority of someone. Jesus was assuming authority over the lives of these two men.

When the two brothers heard His command, they responded immediately. The preaching of John the Baptist had prepared them, but there was something about the way Jesus presented Himself. They sensed that He was the One in control and they should obey!

"Follow" expresses an essential note in Jesus' ministry. It comes as a command but embodies an invitation. It invites those who hear to enter into a personal relationship with the Son of God. To do what these men did is the appropriate response—accept the invitation by following Him. The decision to follow Him is always a faith response. To be a disciple of Jesus is to enjoy His company every day.

We should be encouraged by those whom Jesus first invited into this relationship. Andrew and Peter were not members of the religious establishment, but the working class. They were Galileans, not Judeans. You do not need a religious background to follow Jesus. No references are required!

The promise Jesus attached encouraged a response: "I will make you into fishers of men!" (Mark 1:17). He would do whatever was necessary to include them in His work. He used terms they understood—they knew about fishing. To someone in Atlanta who works as a vice-president in a corporation, Jesus might say, "I will make you a manager in My work of drawing people to Myself." To a bank employee in Dallas, Jesus might say, "I will make you a part of collecting the people who will become My personal treasury." Jesus takes what we know by experience and uses it in the advancement of His work. Jesus will use your background and experience in making you an effective disciple.

your notes

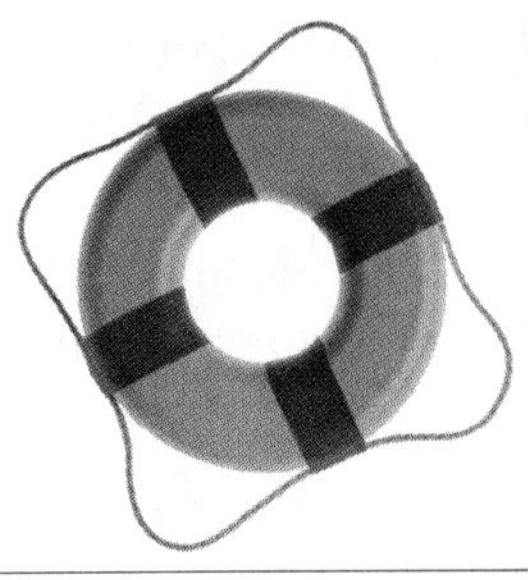

Verse 18 says, "Immediately they left their nets and followed Him." This describes fellowship, companionship, and intimate contact. Soon James and John heard the same command and made the same response (vv. 19-20). Imagine walking side by side with the Son of God and enjoying fellowship with Him daily!

By faith a person enters into a relationship with the living Christ, submits to His control, and joins His community of followers. When Jesus calls us, we must be ready and willing for Him to make us into useful members of His team.

Acknowledge His Control (Mark 1:35-39)

Jesus launched His ministry in Capernaum. He taught with obvious authority. On one occasion a demon-possessed man tried to disrupt Jesus' teaching, but Jesus cast the demon out of the man.

After the synagogue gathering, Jesus went home with Simon (Peter) where He healed Peter's mother-in-law of a fever. In the late evening the people brought victims of all kinds of illnesses to Jesus—and He healed all of them. The disciples were beside themselves with excitement, but the next day was a different story. Jesus confronted the disciples with another challenge.

For Your Consideration

1. Why would Jesus not return to Capernaum with His disciples?

2. In what ways is your church comfortable with the status quo?

When the disciples awakened the next morning, Jesus was missing. After a search they discovered that He had risen early to pray in a deserted place. They said to Him, "Everyone's looking for You" (Mark 1:37). Their plan for the day was set: follow up on yesterday's successes! The success in Capernaum demanded that they build on it something even greater. But Jesus had something else in mind. He had a specific mission to accomplish and if they were to be His disciples, they must adopt it.

Jesus said, "Let's go on to the neighboring villages, so that I may preach there too. This is why I have come" (v. 38). His mission was to take the good news of the kingdom to all the villages of Israel. All the lost sheep of the house of Israel must hear Jesus' message.

your notes

Contemporary followers of Jesus must make the same adjustment. We come to Him with a very limited appreciation of His mission. Usually it does not reach beyond our family and friends. But if we are to follow Jesus, we must adopt His mission—not just to the lost sheep of the house of Israel, but also to every person in every nation (Matt. 28:18-20). You cannot follow Him unless you are prepared to go where He is going. Jesus is working through His church to take the good news to all nations.

Following Jesus will move you outside your comfort zone. One young pastor was distressed to hear the leadership of the church say, "We are not interested in growing as a church. We like things as they are. New people tend to create problems." They were ignoring the mission of Jesus. Those who follow Jesus should share His concern for all to hear.

Maintain His Focus (Mark 2:14-17)

Jesus will constantly surprise you by the things He says and does. The calling of Matthew (Levi) to discipleship was totally unexpected. In the view of many Israelites, when Matthew took a job collecting taxes for the Romans, he sold his soul. How could a faithful Jew work for the hated Romans? Yet Jesus called him, and Matthew went on to write the Gospel that bears his name.

For Your Consideration

1. Why were the religious leaders offended at Jesus' relationship with Matthew?

2. What justification did Jesus use for calling Matthew and his friends?

3. Who would not be welcome in your church next Sunday morning? Why?

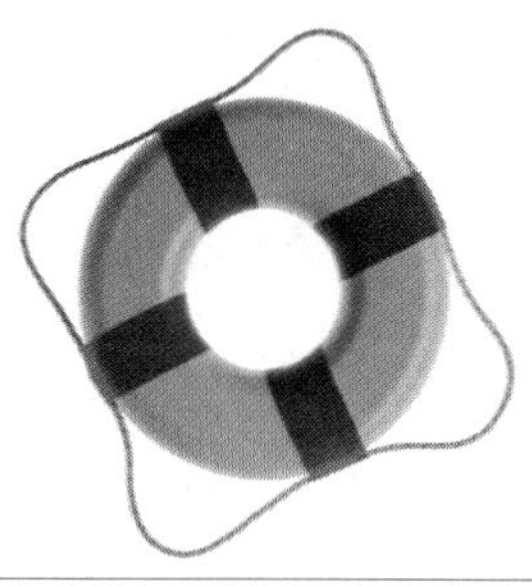

Learning Activity

They Followed Him—Now It's My Turn

Think about the immediate responses of the four disciples in Capernaum and compare them to your response to Jesus' command to follow Him. As you do, answer the following questions:

1. Why did Jesus use the expression "fishers of men" when He called Simon and Andrew?

2. What do you do for a living?

3. Using the way Jesus expressed His call to Simon and Andrew as a guide, how would Jesus express His call to you to follow Him?

4. How has His call to you become more personal now that you have written it this way?

5. How have you responded to His call in your life?

6. How will you respond now?

4. How can you help your church accept the Lord's agenda to reach the lost?

When Jesus called Matthew, he responded just like the first four disciples did—immediately. Even though his friends were outcasts from the circle of the faithful, Matthew wanted them to hear Jesus. So he invited his friends and Jesus to dinner at his home. Jesus shocked the Jewish leadership by accepting the invitation. He did the unthinkable: He actually sat at the same table and shared His message with this unclean crowd. The leaders might admire His deeds of mercy, but they could not accept an agenda that included reaching out to the unclean. This violated their rules!

Jesus defended His action. "Those who are well don't need a doctor, but the sick do need one. I didn't come to call the righteous, but sinners" (Mark 2:17). Jesus did not see the tax collectors as hopeless sinners but as people in need of God's forgiveness. His mission was to offer forgiveness to everyone in society whom others had given up on.

Are you ready to let Jesus set the agenda for your church? What about your personal agenda? I remember a deacon who asked me, as we were preparing to make door-to-door visits, "Pastor, what if a person from another race opens the door?" Even though they had never officially voted on it, the church had an unwritten agenda that excluded a sizable portion of our community. It excluded all persons of color. The deacon was really asking, "Will we follow the agenda of Jesus or the agenda of the culture?"

As the Son of God and Messiah, Jesus is in control. He invites; we respond. He determines the mission; we obey. He sets the agenda; we adjust. John and Cathy, the couple mentioned in the introduction, had it right. If Jesus is in control, we must follow Him!

your notes

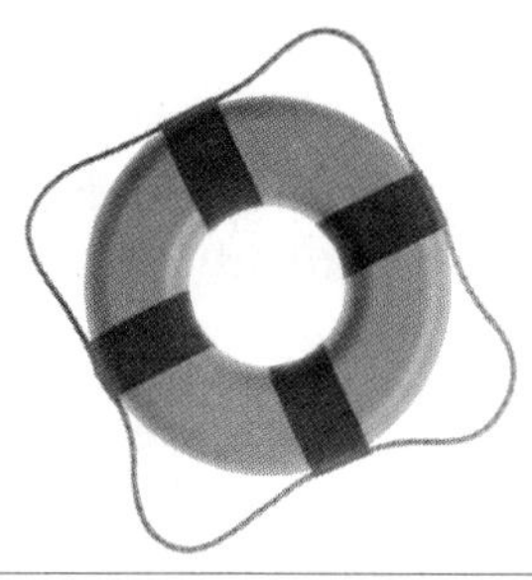

Session 1

What If I Don't Understand?

Scripture Mark 3:7–4:34
Focal: Mark 3:13-19; 4:13-34

My personal journey to faith was relatively simple. Growing up in a home with loving parents and good grandparents—people of faith—made personal faith an easy decision for me. Nothing happened in my early years to make me question the faith of my family. It seemed right at the age of nine to join them in the confession of faith in Jesus as the Son of God, when the Holy Spirit convinced me of my need. My early memories include a church where I experienced the presence of the living Christ in His people and through His Word.

My friend Richard tells a different story. As a child the divorce of his parents shattered his world. The anger and harshness of his father made it difficult to think of God as Father. Then a brother was killed in a tragic accident. The experiences of grief made trust in God very difficult. Richard wondered how a good God could allow so much pain in his life. Also, there was no church in his life. With whose journey do you most closely identify—Richard's or mine?

Jesus was constantly encountering people like Richard who were struggling in their lives. Unfortunately, many gave up their struggles too quickly and surrendered to unbelief. Their prejudices and first impressions kept them from faith. The way Jesus helped the Twelve when they did not understand gives us encouragement that He will help us also.

your notes

Accept Jesus' Call (Mark 3:13-19)

The calling of the Twelve represented a critical turning point in Jesus' ministry. These men would be His official representatives—apostles. He would entrust to them the future of His work in the world.

For Your Consideration

1. What are the names of the twelve apostles? How many did you name on the first try?

2. With which apostle do you find it easy to identify? Why?

3. How would you define *grace*?

4. How does God's call apply to you?

5. What aspect of their call was unique to the Twelve? What does our call have in common with theirs?

After the night of prayer Jesus "summoned those He wanted" to be His disciples (Mark 3:13). The initiative was with Him. The call to salvation and the call to service are at His initiative, and thus they both come by grace.

Take a careful look at the names on the list and grace will be obvious. Notice they are ordinary men! Peter, Andrew, James, and John were fishermen. Matthew was a tax collector, which made him a social and spiritual outcast. Simon, identified as "the Zealot," was probably committed to radical nationalism. The remarkable thing about most of them is that we know nothing about their backgrounds. No genealogy is provided. Most were probably from Galilee and utterly void of any religious training—other than the training provided in Jewish homes and synagogues. They were young and responsive, but

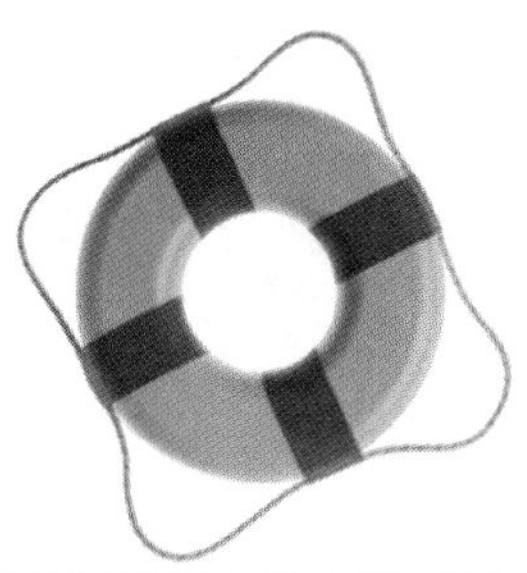

lacking in the training and background you would expect for such an assignment. Grace was at work!

Their flaws and slowness to grow in faith became obvious in the months that followed. The only explanation for Jesus' choice is grace.

Jesus' purpose for the Twelve was threefold: "that they might be with Him and that He might send them out to preach and to have authority to drive out demons" (vv. 14-15). Being "with Him" provided opportunity to grow in their understanding. For three years Jesus taught them, revealed Himself to them, and shared life with them. During that time they were exposed to His heart.

We too are called to such a relationship: "God is faithful: by Him you were called into fellowship with His Son, Jesus Christ our Lord" (1 Cor. 1:9). Fellowship provides the opportunity to understand and suggests the most intimate relationship, like a marriage or a close friendship.

PictureQuest

your notes

From that day forward they were with Him and were available for Him to send them wherever He desired. Jesus sent them out to preach and to cast out demons. "Preach" means "to announce, to proclaim." They delivered the message that He gave as men under His authority. The casting out of the demons in His name demonstrated Jesus' power over Satan's agents and proved that the apostles were indeed His official messengers.

The privilege and mission of the Twelve is now given to the whole church. We have been chosen to have fellowship with Him and to represent Him in the world. We are not given a book of answers to our doubts, but rather the opportunity to be with Him in His work. As we accept His call to join Him in the work, an understanding of His will and ways develops.

Develop Your Capacity to Hear (Mark 4:13-20)

Jesus adopted parables as an effective way to communicate His message. Parables make comparisons to aid understanding. As a boy I learned, "a parable is an earthly story with a heavenly meaning," which is a good definition. Jesus used everyday experiences to illustrate spiritual truths.

The parable of the soils compares the heart to four kinds of soil and the gospel to seeds. Jesus used this to encourage a proper response to His message. The four kinds of soil describe four ways that people respond to the gospel.

For Your Consideration

1. Why is a "seed" such an appropriate figure for the gospel?

2. What made it easy for Satan to take the word away so quickly?

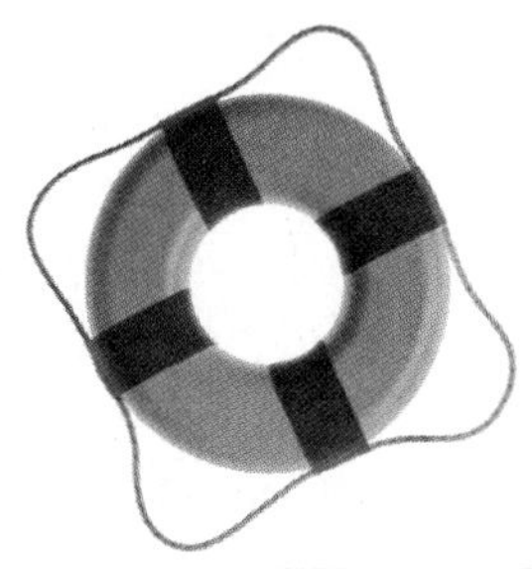

3. Which of the three things listed in verse 19 has hindered the Word most in your life? How have you addressed this problem?

4. What determines the fruitfulness of the Word in our lives? What are the differences reflected in the 30, 60, and 100?

All four soil types refer to people who heard the word. Even the person represented by the hardened path heard the word. But the hardened hearer paid no attention to what he heard. Satan took it away before it could take root in the heart (v. 15) The second also heard and even received the word in a shallow way. The response of the shallow person was emotional and temporary. The word was abandoned the first time it began to cost them something (v. 17). The third also heard, but not with a pure heart. The seed could never become fruitful because of the inner distractions (v. 19). Listen carefully to the word if you want it to make a difference (v. 20)!

Three of the four hearers welcomed the word. Even the shallow hearer received it "with joy" (v. 16). But only the good soil (the good hearer) allowed the seed to take root, to really find a place in the heart.

The proper welcome involves allowing the word to bring about changes in your life, even to produce good fruit. The third type of hearer came close, but in the end other things kept the word from producing a crop. The things that hindered the word were "the worries of this age, the pleasure of wealth, and the desires for other things" (v. 19). By today's standards, the list sounds reasonable. But anything that prevents trust and obedience is fatal to fruitfulness.

Agriculture dominates the scene in our part of Texas. Watching the farmers prepare the soil for sowing is interesting. They plow, dig, fertilize, apply chemicals, and then irrigate, and all these activities are just in preparation for the sowing. If we really want to understand the things of God, we can prepare our hearts as the farmer prepares the field. The seed is powerful and the Sower is faithful, but the condition of the soil is our responsibility.

In our response to the gospel our fruitfulness will vary (v. 20). Some will be multiplied 30 times, some 60, and some a 100. Our giftedness and opportunities will determine the extent of the multiplication, but we can be equal in our wholehearted response to the message of the gospel.

your notes

Act on What You Understand (Mark 4:21-25)

Even though it may not be immediately obvious, the parable of the lamp is about hearing the word and relates to the parable of the soils. Followers of Jesus are to use all of the truth they receive from Him.

For Your Consideration

1. How is the gospel like light?

2. How do you apply the gospel to your daily life?

3. What is the reward for sharing the light we have received?

4. What happened the last time you shared the light you have received?

Where do you place a lamp? You do not place it under a basket or under a bed—this would probably set them on fire. Rather, you would use a shelf or a stand made especially for the lamp.

The lamp represents the truth the disciples received from Jesus. It is not to be stored away but applied to

A CLOSER LOOK

The Gospel

Produces fruit like a seed (4:8).
Reveals like a lamp (4:21,22).
Blesses when shared (4:24,25).
Demonstrates the power of the kingdom of God (4:26-29).
Defies human calculation (4:30-32).

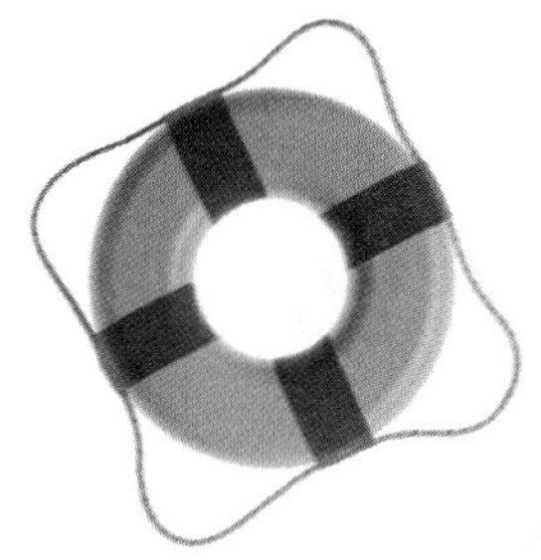

life. When we hear the word, it can be useful to us. We are to live in the light of what we have heard. To hear the word and not apply it to life is like putting the lamp under the bed. Don't hide it; use it in your family, your business, and your personal life!

Measures were used in the marketplace where grain was bought and sold. Jesus sometimes used it to warn about the seriousness of life—that on the day of reckoning the Judge will weigh the measure of judgment we have been using to criticize others. Here Jesus used it to encourage us to share what we have received. It is not enough just to be a good hearer of the word; we must be faithful in measuring out to others what we have understood. The principle Jesus set forth is that when we share what we understand, we increase our capacity to understand.

Jesus said, "Pay attention to what you hear" (v. 24). Pay attention as you did the first time your heard a flight attendant give her instructions. Remember? You may never need what she said, but you still needed to listen just in case. Jesus' message is critical for your life. You need it today and will have opportunity to share it with others who need it also.

Be Patient as You Work (Mark 4:26-32)

There is always a supernatural dimension to the kingdom of God; there is more going on than the eye can see. Jesus sometimes spoke of the kingdom of God as the future hope of the people of God, and at other times as a present reality. Here Jesus emphasized the present reality of the kingdom with two parables that involve seeds. The first parable emphasizes a process and the second power. Both point to the present activity of God.

For Your Consideration

1. What did Jesus mean by "the kingdom of God"?

2. How can we experience the kingdom of God today?

3. How is the final judgment like a harvest?

4. What is the primary lesson of the parable of the mustard seed?

your notes

5. How have you observed the power and the process of God's work in your church?

6. How do you explain the life-changing power of the gospel?

7. What can you learn from the parable about your personal ministry? about the ministry of your church?

8. Where have you seen the power of the kingdom at work in your world?

Followers of Jesus learn to trust the process like a good farmer (vv. 26-27). A farmer sows the seeds and then goes about his daily life. He sleeps, takes care of

Learning Activity

More About Jesus

What are you going to do so you can *learn* more about Jesus and His teachings?

What are you going to do so you can *share* more about Jesus and His teachings?

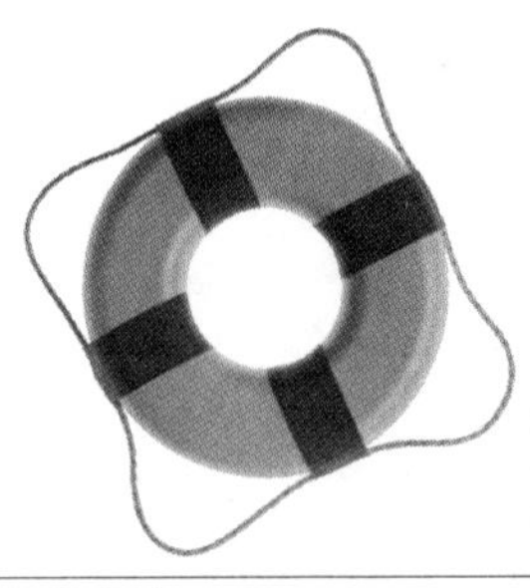

Learning Activity

Soil Analysis

In Jesus' interpretation of the parable of the soils in Mark 4:13-20, He taught that each of the soils describes various ways people respond to His Word. Fill in the blanks for each of the four soils in the passage.

1. __________________ ground relates to a __________________ hearer.

   How would you describe this obstacle to hearing God's Word?

2. __________________ ground relates to a __________________ hearer.

   How would you describe this obstacle to hearing God's Word?

3. __________________ ground relates to a __________________ hearer.

   How would you describe this obstacle to hearing God's Word?

4. __________________ ground relates to a __________________ hearer.

   How would describe this environment for hearing God's Word?

Answers:

1 **Hard** ground relates to a **cold, indifferent** hearer.
2. Rocky ground relates to a **rootless** hearer.
3. **Thorny** ground relates to a **worldly** hearer.
4. **Good** ground relates to a **responsive** hearer.

his responsibilities, and trusts the seeds to do what only the seeds can do. While the farmer is sleeping and pursuing other interests, the seeds are sprouting and growing—and the farmer does not know how! Yet the soil produces a crop that is gathered in the harvest. "The soil produces a crop by itself—first the blade, then the head, and then the ripe grain on the head. But as soon as the crop is ready, he sends for the sickle, because harvest has come" (vv. 28-29). One can be a good farmer without understanding the scientific explanations about what makes seeds grow. He simply trusts the process.

This is way the seed works in our hearts. The growth of grace and the production of fruit in our lives is a process—the Lord works it out in us. The Word of truth is received in our lives and God works through this Word to make our lives productive. He finishes what He starts (Phil. 1:6). This is also the way the Lord works with the seed we sow. We have the privilege of working with Him in sowing the seed in the hearts of others, but we have to trust the process. The gospel is "God's power for salvation to everyone who believes" (Rom. 1:16).

Jesus' audience was familiar with the little mustard seed. It was the smallest seed the gardener sowed in his garden and yet it could become a small tree. It would usually grow to 6 or 7 feet tall and would occasionally even reach 12 feet. When you look at the mustard seed, there is nothing to suggest that it can grow to such strength and height that even birds can roost in it, but it does. There is a principle of life at work in the seed.

The word of the kingdom is like that! Outwardly it may not appear to have much promise, but when it is sown in the soil of a human heart, it has the potential to make great things happen. It has the life of God in it. This should encourage those who are called to sow the seed in difficult places. There is power in the seed of the Word.

None of us will ever fully understand the ways of God in salvation. It is not necessary to understand

your notes

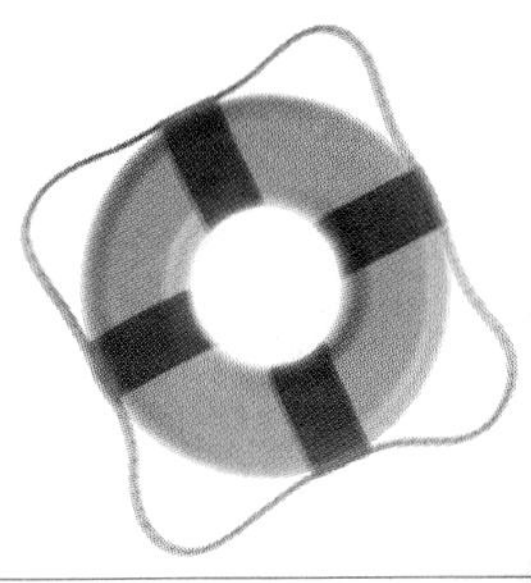

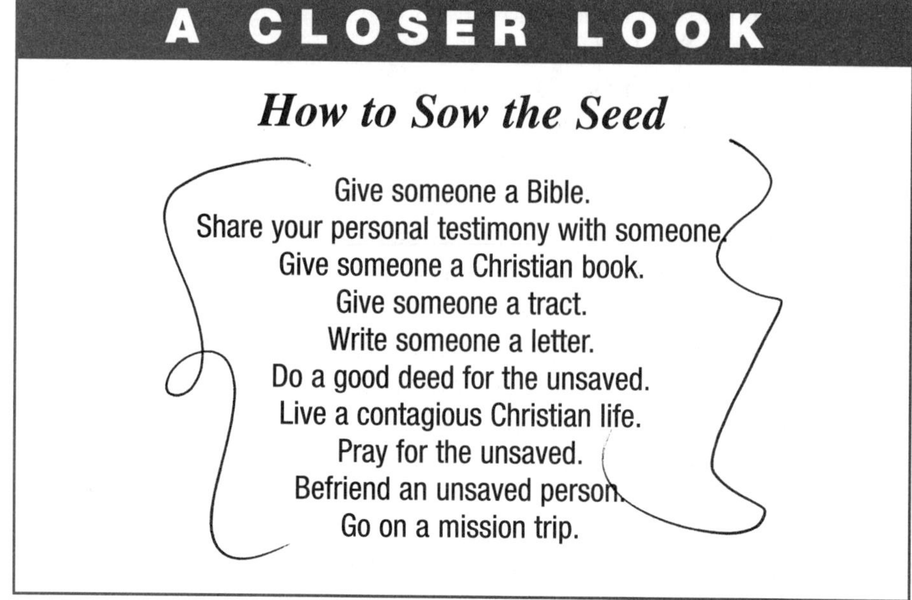

everything in order to be saved or to participate in the spread of the gospel. We can share the gospel without fully understanding how God uses it to bring about the new birth. Just trust the process and the power. Even though we do not understand certain things, we still take advantage of the opportunities that come our way. Spiritually, these may include the opportunity to respond to Jesus' call, welcome His Word, and be involved in His work.

Depend on Jesus to Help You (Mark 4:33-34)

Sometimes Jesus' parables are hard for us to understand, and the Twelve found them difficult to grasp as well. But Jesus spoke these parables to communicate important spiritual truths, and His followers need to learn these truths so they can serve Him better.

For Your Consideration

1. Why did Jesus speak in parables so often?

2. How should the parables in this study affect the way you live?

3. Do you look to Jesus to help you understand His teachings?

your notes

PictureQuest

Jesus often spoke in parables as part of His instructions to the disciples, but He did not leave them in the dark about what the parables meant. The disciples misunderstood Jesus on numerous occasions, so it is not surprising that they found the parables puzzling as well. But after teaching them through parables, Jesus "would explain everything" (v. 34) to them. James Brooks explained: "Again Mark emphasized the necessity of understanding. A better translation of the last part of verse 33 may be 'in a way they could understand.' The first sentence in v. 34 applies only to a particular occasion, not to Jesus' entire ministry. It does, however, reflect Mark's view that everything Jesus taught was an enigma to those who were hostile or indifferent."[1]

Followers of Jesus have an obligation to study Jesus' parables. We must not only strive to understand these passages but learn to apply them to our lives in a way that pleases Him.

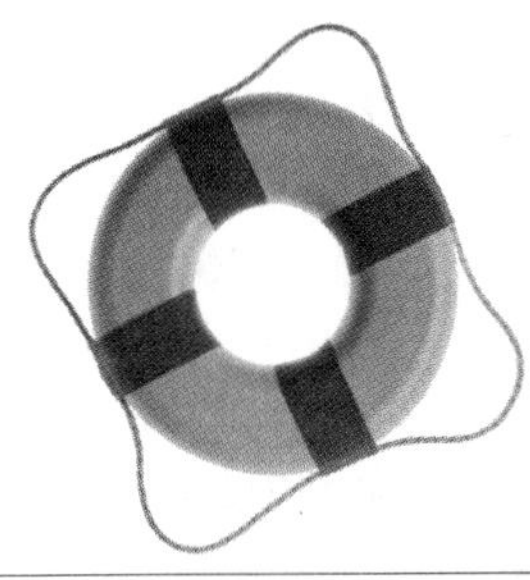

---

[1]James A. Brooks, "Mark" in *The New American Commentary* (Nashville: Broadman Press, 1991), p. 86.

Session 2

What Can I Do?

Scripture **Mark 4:35–6:56**
Focal: Mark 6:7–13,30–44

God works through ordinary people. Irene Curtis stands out in my mind as an ordinary person who served God in extraordinary ways. She was a widow, retired from a good job, and could have lived in a very comfortable home. Instead she chose to live in an old hotel not far from our church. The hotel had been the pride of the city 70 years earlier, but was now home to the homeless and troubled. Her son-in-law was the minister of music in the largest Baptist church in the world, and he told his wife about his concern for Mrs. Curtis's welfare.

Why did she choose to live in the hotel? The jail was just around the corner; she visited there regularly. The hospitals were within walking distance; she ministered there almost daily. The bus station was nearby; she traveled by bus. The church was around another corner; she never missed. Wherever she went, she gave Bibles, passed out tracts, witnessed to people, offered a prayer, and met physical needs. This frail little grandmother was on mission for the Lord. Has Jesus given you your assignment? He does have something you can do! We learn this from the way He worked in the lives of His first disciples. In this study we will discover that God has a place of ministry and a vital role in that ministry for every one of His children to fulfill. If you are not involved in a ministry as you should be, this study will provide you with a great opportunity to discover what God wants you to do—and the encouragement to do it!

GO! (MARK 6:7-13)

your notes

Jesus opened another phase of His ministry with the sending of the Twelve. While the instructions given to these men were unique to their situation, these instructions also inform us. The Lord commands all of us to go (Matt. 28:19-20).

For Your Consideration

1. What would be the benefits of going two by two?

2. Would you agree that fear is a great hindrance in doing the work of evangelism today? Would having a partner help?

3. How would you define "authority" in this context?

4. Do demons still possess people? If so, what does this mean for our task as witnesses?

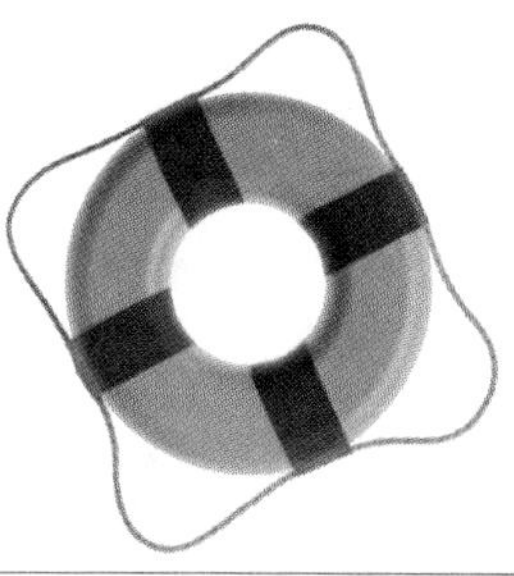

Learning Activity

Striking a Balance

Mark 6 indicates that Christians should strike a balance between *going* and *resting* as we serve Jesus our Lord. Balancing those two disciplines can be difficult. Perhaps looking at the ways you express both of these important commands can be a good place to start. Reflect on your daily or weekly schedule in light of Jesus' commands and evaluate yourself.

How do you express your willingness to *go*? (Read Mark 6:7-13 before you answer.)

How do you express your willingness to *rest*? (Read Mark 6:30-32 before you answer.)

How do you need to change your schedule so you can find the necessary balance between *going* and *resting*?

your notes

5. What does it mean to "shake the dust off" one's feet? When would it be appropriate for Christians to do that? Why?

6. What factors make the task of evangelism urgent in our day? How should this affect us?

Jesus followed a Jewish principle in sending the Twelve in pairs. This principle was based on the law of Moses, which stated that at least two witnesses were needed to confirm a fact in court (see Deut. 17:6). The Greeks followed the same principle when an important mission was at stake. It is interesting that the best evangelism strategies of our day have found it wise to send witnesses out as members of a team of two or three. The highly effective FAITH Sunday School Evangelism Strategy® sends people out to witness with three on each team.

When two go together, they encourage each other. In this case six teams were better than twelve individuals carrying the gospel. I remember two laymen who became partners in witnessing. They agreed to go out one night each week and share the gospel with as many people as possible. Bill managed an auto dealership, and Joe owned and managed an auto auction company. Over several years they shared the message with hundreds and saw many become faithful followers of Christ. They kept each other going.

Jesus "gave them authority" (Mark 6:7). As His representatives, the Twelve could use Jesus' name when they encountered lives under demonic control. Jesus' authority would be with them for the whole mission. Although demons have frightening power, they are no match for the name of Jesus. His authority extended to the very powers of darkness. At His word they had to leave their victims. The Twelve experienced the power of His name as they exercised His authority that had been delegated to them.

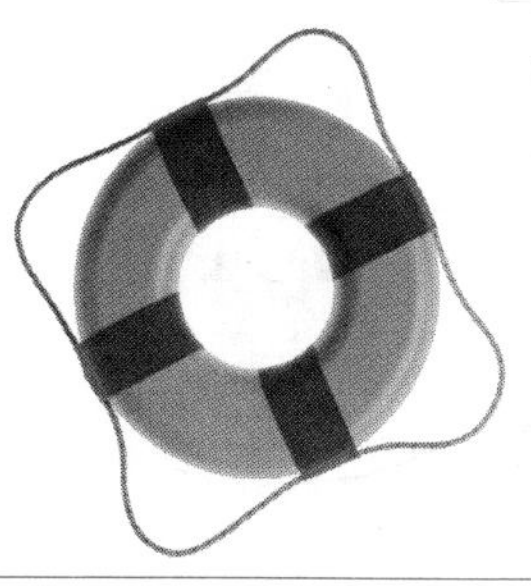

We also go in Jesus' name and under His authority. We have the power of the Holy Spirit to make us effective witnesses (Acts 1:8). Jesus' commission gives us the status of an official ambassador of the King (see 2 Cor. 5:20). Later Jesus promised, "And remember, I am with you always, to the end of the age" (Matt. 28:20).

Jesus "instructed them to take nothing for the road except a walking stick: no bread, no backpack, no money in their belts, but to wear sandals, and not to put on an extra shirt" (Mark 6:8-9). More than the essentials would slow them down.

Neither rejection nor resistance should delay the Twelve on this mission. They were to indicate the seriousness of their task by shaking "the dust off [their] feet as a testimony against them" (v. 11). The rejection was not a personal affront; the listeners had rejected the message from the King. Jesus knew that the time for His ministry was limited, so He urged haste as they carried out their assignment. They had to keep moving!

The Twelve were to take no extra food or clothing with them because those they helped would meet their needs. While these instructions applied specifically to the assignment of the Twelve, the urgency applies to all of us. Like their Lord, the Twelve went out ministering and preaching. They called on the hearers to repent, even as they drove out demons and healed the sick (v. 12). The anointing with oil may have been an aid for faith or it may have been applied for medicinal purposes (v. 13). Since the anointing was connected with healing, it seems that it was an aid to faith and represented the work of the Holy Spirit in healing.

We too can go and share the good news. We have all we need in Christ and in the power of the Holy Spirit. We can go as official ambassadors of the King of kings.

Rest! (Mark 6:30-32)

Here we see the wisdom of Jesus as a leader. Even though the disciples were on an emotional high after their first missionary trip, Jesus knew they were vulnerable. He knew it was time to take them to a place of solitude so they could maintain physical and spiritual wholeness. It was time to "rest."

For Your Consideration

1. How could you encourage your pastor and staff to get proper rest?

2. How important is rest to your spiritual health?

3. Why were there always crowds around Jesus and His disciples?

4. How do you make sure that you have enough rest to maintain your spiritual health?

5. Give your definition of "rest" in verse 31.

King Herod became aware of the missionary efforts of the Twelve and mistakenly thought Jesus, in whose name the apostles preached, was John returned from the dead (Mark 6:14-16). It was not necessarily a good thing to have this king interested in what they were doing. His interest in the ministry of John the Baptist had resulted in the death of the faithful prophet (vv. 16-29). Jesus was aware of the threat Herod was to the work and the problems his opposition could cause for Him and His disciples. This situation was one of the factors that prompted Jesus to arrange for a time of rest.

While stress is normal, too much stress over an extended period can be a threat to body and spirit. Both body and spirit require relief from pressure so their strength can be renewed. Military leaders provide periods of rest and relaxation for fighting forces. The Leader of the Twelve realized the same need in His workers.

The report of the Twelve was good! His ministry and their work had created so much excitement that it was hard to "even have time to eat" (v. 31). While this can be exhilarating, it also takes a toll in emotional energy. You have emotional and physical limitations, so renewal through rest is required.

Some people in full-time ministry have wrongly exempted themselves from such limitations. They ignore their own humanity to their own detriment. They need to learn from our Lord who arranged an away time so He and the apostles would be at their best

your notes

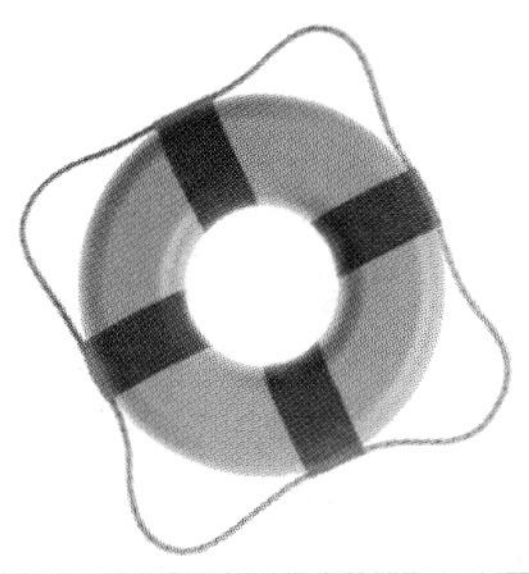

on another day. In addition to a weekly Sabbath, we occasionally need extended rest to maintain our health and to enhance our usefulness.

CARE! (MARK 6:33-44)

The crowds would not allow Jesus to rest. To the very end of His life they kept coming. His compassion drew them, even if His disciples were often less responsive. When the crowds came, Jesus ministered to them and His disciples learned.

For Your Consideration

1. Why is the care of a shepherd so critical for sheep?

A CLOSER LOOK

The Shepherd

Instead of being "sheep without a shepherd" (Mark 6:34), we as Christians can turn to the Lord to be our shepherd. This is what King David described so beautifully in Psalm 23 about 3,000 years ago:

The LORD is my shepherd; there is nothing I lack.
He lets me lie down in green pastures;
He leads me beside quiet waters.
He renews my life;
He leads me along the right paths for His name's sake.
Even when I walk through the darkest valley,
I fear no danger, for You are with me;
Your rod and Your staff—they comfort me.
You prepare a table before me in the presence of my enemies;
You anoint my head with oil;
my cup overflows.
Only goodness and faithful love will pursue me
all the days of my life,
and I will dwell in the house of the LORD as long as I live.

2. How do you explain Jesus' compassion toward human needs?

3. When was the last time you were moved from your heart to help a person in need? How did it affect you?

4. Why were the disciples so slow to respond to the hunger of the crowd?

5. If I tithe through my church, does it relieve me from responsibility for needs I may encounter during the week? Why or why not?

6. What was the nature of the miracle in the multiplication of the loaves?

Jesus saw something His disciples missed. He saw that "they were like sheep without a shepherd" (v. 34). In the Old Testament the shepherd was the model of the ideal leader. A good leader cares about the welfare of the people just as a shepherd cares for his sheep. The Lord is ever the Shepherd to His people (Ps. 23:1). The political and religious leaders had failed the people, and Jesus "had compassion on them" (Mark 6:34). Compassion is a deep emotional response of tenderness and care for those in need. Watch Jesus' response to the crowd, and you will know how deeply He cared.

Look at the crowds around you! What do you see? Do you see children from broken homes, rebellious youth, uncaring moms, delinquent dads? Do you see people who desperately need a Shepherd? Followers of Jesus must begin to see people in the crowds the way Jesus saw them—lost sheep in need of a loving Shepherd.

Unshepherded is not an actual term, but it is better than *unchurched* to describe the lost. It means that there is no one looking out for their spiritual needs—

your notes

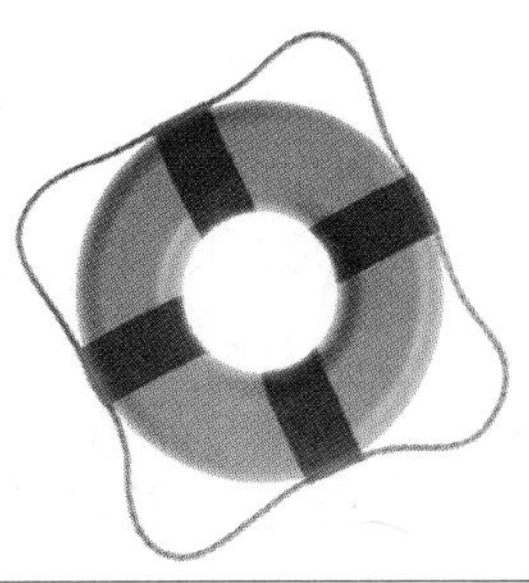

no one is praying for them, relieving their pain, ministering to their needs. Referring to the lost as if they are simply prospects for local churches does not address the depth of their needs or the true mission of the church.

Jesus' disciples considered the crowd to be a problem. They admonished Jesus to send them away when it was time to eat. But Jesus had different plans. He said, "You give them something to eat" (v. 37). The disciples' reaction was predictable. Jesus was asking them to do the impossible. They told Jesus it would take "200 denarii worth of bread" to give each person a little. One denarius was the expected wage for a hard day's work! No one in the group had that kind of money.

But Jesus was not persuaded by their argument. He asked, "How many loaves do you have? Go look." After a search they found "five, and two fish" (v. 38). These were actually the meal that a mother had prepared for a youngster that morning (John 6:9). The loaves were probably flat barley loaves eaten by the peasants in that area, and the fish were likely small fish that had been dried and salted. Not much to start with when you have several thousand people to feed!

However, the lad and the disciples made the food available to Jesus. This is what we do when we care. We put what we have in the hands of our mighty Lord and allow Him to use it to meet needs.

Billions of dollars are not required in God's economy. Someone has wisely said, "Little is much when God is in it." The availability of what we have is enough! Remember, this was an assignment for the disciples as a group—"you" in Mark 6:37 is a plural pronoun. We should join fellow believers and the Lord in responding to the needs we see.

Ordinarily the disciples did nothing more than observe while Jesus performed His miracles, but this situation was different. In this case Jesus included them in the miracle—He wanted them to do what they could. They made the search that found the five loaves and two fish. They arranged the crowd into companies of hundreds and fifties. After Jesus blessed the small provisions, the disciples received it from His hands as it multiplied and then distributed it to the people. They gathered up the twelve full baskets of food that were left over. Their contribution may seem small, but it was significant.

When we do what we can, the Lord does more than we ever could. Jesus performed the miracle of causing five loaves and two fish to multiply so there was enough food to feed thousands of people. Surely the

One who created grain and fish in the beginning was able to cause such multiplication for a specific need.

Many years ago First Baptist Church in Lubbock, Texas, made a commitment to an inner city ministry in the midst of a major remodeling program. This decision strained all of our financial resources. It did not

Learning Activity

Care Packages

Serving the Lord involves caring for people's needs in ways they can touch and see. Answer these questions prayerfully, asking God to open your eyes to the needs He wants you to meet.

1. What are some of the needs among the people in your church?

2. What are some of the needs among the people in your community?

3. What are some of the ways you can meet those needs?

4. What are you going to ask Jesus to provide so you can meet those needs?

your notes

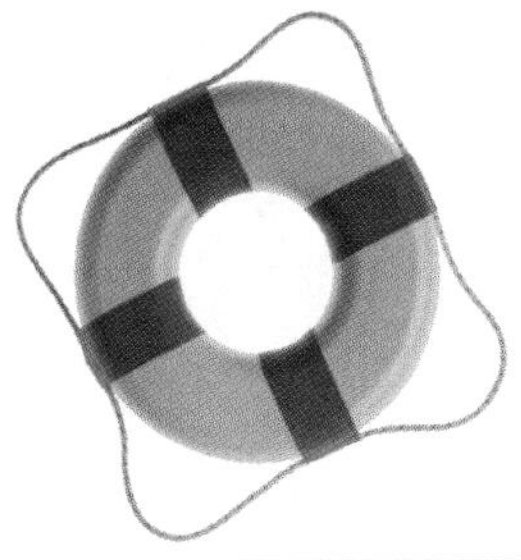

make any sense at all—financially at least—but God had placed us in the midst of so much human need. We committed ourselves to Him and began to look to Him for provisions. We experienced one timely miracle after another. A building became available through an inner city church that was disbanding. The will of a godly lady who had recently died provided money for needed repairs to the building. From Sunday School classes and even other churches, volunteers stepped forward. Soon food and clothing were available. Teachers and resources for a Christian Women's Job Corp program emerged. Soon a pastor came on the scene to start an inner city church in the center. On and on it went and continues today. When we care enough to act, we experience the limitless resources of our Lord.

A principle we must learn from this experience is that we must not wait until we have the resources in hand to begin. Jesus multiplied the loaves even as they were being distributed. The main question concerns your assignment. Have you received it? For Irene Curtis, the woman mentioned in the introduction, it was in an old hotel in the inner city. Jesus assigns each of His followers a place where they can make a difference.

PictureQuest

Session 2

CHAPTER 4

Who Can Help Me?

Scripture **Mark 7:1–8:26**
Focal: Mark 8:1–10,14–26

Some remarkable reports of God's saving work are coming out of the prisons of America. Charles Colson is one notable example. As a member of President Richard Nixon's White House staff, he broke the law and served time in prison. He fell from the heights of political power to the shame of imprisonment. On his way to prison a friend shared with him the gospel of Jesus Christ and assured him that God loved him. When he prayed a simple prayer of faith and repentance, he experienced the new birth. It was the beginning of a whole new life that has brought about an effective prison ministry.

Most of those finding Christ in prison are not as famous as Charles Colson. More of them are like Jan Payne. She was jailed for selling and using drugs. Before being caught, she had built a reputation of violence and hardness.

Her bent to violence continued in jail and landed her in solitary confinement. This provided an opportunity to read a New Testament that someone had given her. The Bible created hope in her troubled heart! If Jesus is who the Bible says He is, maybe He would help her. When she turned to Him with a desperate prayer, He did help her. Like Colson, Jan also became a new creation and has been involved in a local prison ministry.

As this study's larger context reminds us, Jesus understood the depth of human need. Whether He was ministering to religious leaders or a Gentile woman near Sidon, He knew that the problem with humanity is in the human heart (Mark 7:1-30). Jesus never met an impossible situation—not even someone who could neither hear nor speak clearly (vv. 31-37). By taking a careful look at two of Jesus' miracles and one of His teaching situations, we can discover for ourselves the One who can help us.

The Compassionate Jesus (Mark 8:1-10)

The crowds kept coming with their problems! Jesus so captivated this crowd with His teaching ministry that they were reluctant to go home. After three days the food supply was exhausted. When Jesus saw their situation, He said: "I have compassion on the crowd" (v. 2). This was normal for Him! The sight of human need moved something in Him and prompted Him to meet the need.

For Your Consideration

1. Why were the citizens of the Decapolis considered unclean by the leaders in Jerusalem?
2. What distinguishes this feeding miracle from the one recorded in Mark 6:30-44?
3. What does the compassion of Jesus mean to you personally? How does it affect your attitude toward Him?
4. What significance would you give to the fact that this miracle was at the initiative of Jesus?
5. Why did Mark report exactly how much food was left over?
6. Why did the disciples not expect Him to feed this crowd since He had fed the five thousand?

Who were these people that moved Jesus so deeply? While the text does not actually indicate their location or identify the people involved, the larger context puts them on the eastern side of the

your notes

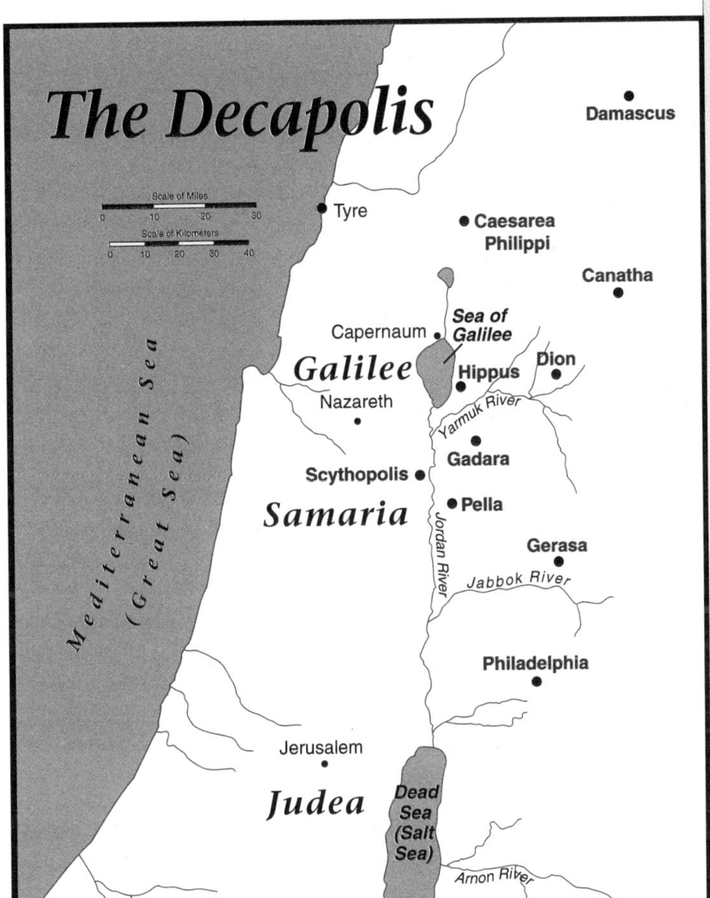

Jordan. His journey to Tyre and Sidon had taken Him outside the land of Israel (7:24), and it seems He then went to the region of Decapolis (7:31). The population there was a mixture of Jews and Gentiles, and the leaders in Jerusalem considered them unclean. About 4 thousand men, giving a total of about 12 thousand, sat at His table this time. They may not have been on the approved list in Jerusalem, but Jesus was moved by their needs. The fact that they were social outcasts and considered spiritually unclean did not bother Him.

This should encourage all of us! We may not be worthy of His attention, but He does care about our needs, even our physical ones.

Learning Activity

Miraculous Comparisons

Read the two stories in Mark about Jesus' miraculously feeding the crowds of people (Mark 6:30-44; 8:1-10). After you have read both stories, answer the following questions by placing a T for true or F for false in the blanks.

____ 1. Jesus fed 4,000 people in the first miracle and 5,000 people in the second miracle.

____ 2. Jesus was moved by compassion in the first miracle but not the second miracle.

____ 3. By the second miracle, Jesus' disciples had learned to respond differently to the people's need for something to eat.

____ 4. In the first miracle the disciples collected 12 baskets of food, but in the second miracle they collected 7 baskets of food.

____ 5. In both miracles, the persons who gave the loaves and fish are identified.

____ 6. In the second miracle, the people had been with Jesus for three days.

____ 7. In both miracles, Jesus instructed the people to sit down on the ground.

____ 8. After the first miracle Jesus dismissed the crowd, but after the second miracle Jesus continued to teach the people.

____ 9. After both miracles, Jesus instructed the disciples to get into a boat.

____10. Between the first and second miracles, the disciples showed a marked improvement in their understanding that Jesus is Lord.

Answers:

1.F 2.F 3.F 4.T 5.F 6.T 7.T 8.F 9.T 10.F

your notes

The hungry crowd did not ask Jesus for help. The dull disciples did not even consider the possibility of His feeding the crowd. This is surprising since they had witnessed the feeding of an even larger group a few months earlier (6:35-44). Jesus noticed the hunger and set in motion the miracle of the loaves. The disciples thought that the distance was too great to bring food to such an isolated place (8:4).

Jesus asked, "How many loaves do you have?" (v. 5). He pointed them first to the resources they had for such an emergency. They had seven loaves of bread. They were enough! Just as He had used what was available in the previous miracle of feeding, He used the seven loaves this time.

The pattern for the miracle was the same: "Taking the seven loaves, He gave thanks, broke the loaves, and kept on giving them to His disciples to set before them" (v. 6). Jesus did more than "feel" their need; He acted. He took what was available and met the crowd's need.

"A few small fish" were found (v. 7), so the crowd had a normal meal—loaves and fish. When the meal was finished, there were "seven large baskets of left-over pieces" (v. 8). These were not just leftover crumbs, but food that was never served.

Jesus responds to needs wherever they may occur. As usual Jesus met the need without setting any conditions. It was an act of pure mercy for Him to set before this religiously mixed crowd such an abundant meal. When Jesus fed the hungry crowd so freely and fully, He revealed the heart of God. God does care about you and the needs you are experiencing in your life! He can help you!

The religious leaders of Israel persisted in their unbelief. Even though Jesus taught the greatest lessons ever heard and performed miracle after miracle, they wanted more. They demanded a sign from heaven before they would believe. They wanted more than a healing miracle, or the feeding of the crowd. They

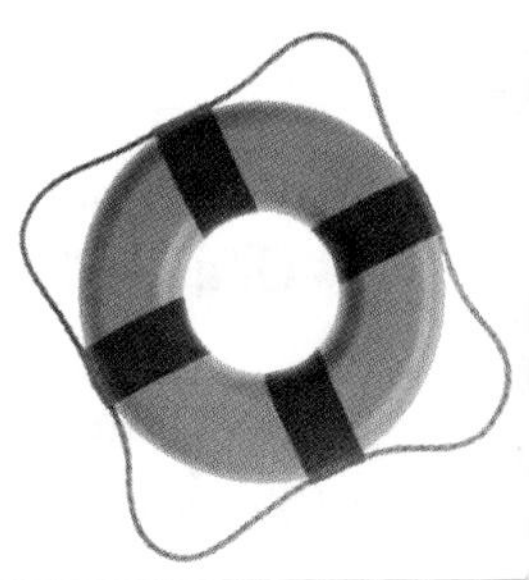

demanded that Jesus perform a sign, some display in nature like the stopping of the sun (as Joshua did) or like calling down fire from heaven (as Elijah did). They demanded that it be "from heaven" (that is, from God), thus authenticating Jesus' claims.

Even though the leaders' unbelief caused Him deep pain, Jesus did not grant their demand. Rather, with a deep sigh from His heart, He said, "Why does this generation demand a sign? I assure you: No sign will be given to this generation!" (v. 12). He did not call down fire from heaven or cause the earth to open up and swallow them as happened to the wilderness generation that rejected the leadership of Moses. Instead, He left the door of faith open to them—but on His terms, not theirs. O what divine patience!

The Patient Jesus (Mark 8:14-21)

Jesus found more faith among the Gentiles than He did in Israel. Consider the mother He met in the region of Tyre and Sidon (Mark 7:24-30). She had enough faith to approach Jesus about her daughter who was demon possessed. She even had enough faith to persist in pressing for a response when Jesus appeared reluctant to respond to her appeal. In the end her faith was rewarded by the deliverance of her daughter (v. 30). But in Israel it was different!

For Your Consideration

1. What did the Pharisees teach that Jesus considered dangerous to His disciples?

2. What would you identify in this passage as evidence of Jesus' patience?

3. How were the disciples different from the unbelieving generation that demanded a sign?

4. What application does this passage have for us? Are we missing what God is saying to us?

Jesus moved away from the unbelieving Jewish leaders but then offered a warning to His disciples. "Watch out! Beware of the yeast of the Pharisees and the yeast of Herod" (v. 15). The teachings and attitudes of these two groups posed a serious threat to the disciples. They represented the prevailing attitudes of the culture—unbelief and worldliness.

The disciples were so preoccupied with their present circumstance that they totally misunderstood. When they heard "yeast," they thought of bread. When they thought of bread, they remembered that they had failed to bring any food for the trip. They thought Jesus was warning them to remember to have enough bread for their meals at all times.

Can you not imagine Jesus' frustration? He gave a solemn warning about a serious spiritual threat, and the disciples misunderstood Him completely. Every teacher can identify with Jesus. Jesus did not give up on them, however, but dealt with them in patience.

The Lord used six questions to confront the disciples' spiritual dullness. "Why are you discussing that you do not have any bread?" (v. 17) Even though they had not asked Him about the bread, He knew about their discussion and concern. "Do you not yet understand or comprehend?" (v. 17). They would have to acknowledge their lack of comprehension. "Is your heart hardened?" (v. 17). They would remember the lesson Jesus had given the Pharisees on the heart when they criticized Him for failing to cleanse His hands before eating. Jesus had explained to the disciples just how critical the heart is (7:1-23), whether in our worship of God or in our everyday behavior. Evil begins in the heart. A hardened heart is not responsive to the truth of God.

Jesus echoed the words of an Old Testament prophet when He asked, "Do you have eyes, and not see, and do you have ears, and not hear?" (8:18). Then He stirred their memories: "And do you not remember?" (v. 18). Had they forgotten so soon that the powers of the kingdom were at work in Him? The Lord went over

your notes

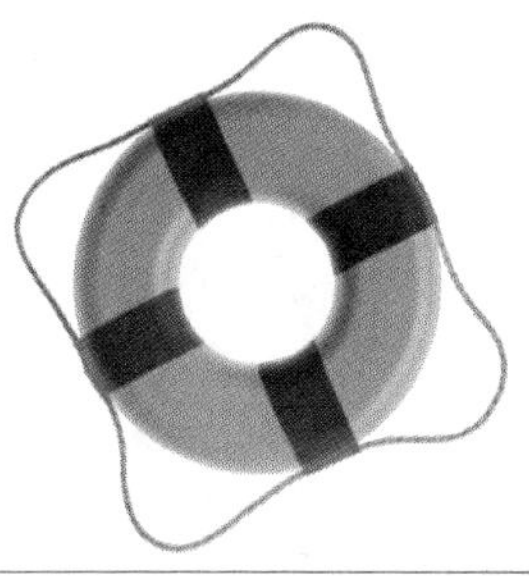

Learning Activity

I Must Tell Jesus

As you put yourself in the place of the blind man who came to Jesus for healing, think about the following areas in your relationship with Him.

Situations in which I trusted Him . . .

How He responded to me . . .

Situations in which I need to trust Him more . . .

What I will do if He responds instantly . . .

What I will do if He responds gradually . . .

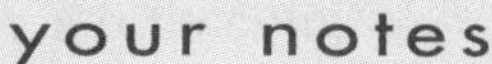

the details of the recent events. How many baskets of food were left over when the crowds had been fed? He closed with a final question: "Don't you understand yet?" (v. 21). The question in the Greek text expects an affirmative answer. Jesus was commending the understanding that they had, but He was also reminding them there was room for improvement!

Can you identify with these slow-learning disciples? Thank God for the patience of the Lord Jesus. He is always nudging us toward an enlarged understanding of who He is and what He is doing in the world.

THE POWERFUL JESUS (MARK 8:22-26)

Only Mark reported this miracle. The disciples received another example of the power of Jesus and of His readiness to meet our needs.

For Your Consideration

1. What evidence do we have of the faith of those who brought the blind man to Jesus?

2. Would you bring a friend to Jesus if he had such a problem? Why or why not?

3. Why did Jesus spit in the man's eyes?

4. Do you agree that the miracle is also a parable of the condition of the disciples—that they needed a second touch? Why or why not?

Shortly afterward, "They brought a blind man to Him and begged Him to touch him" (v. 22). "They" likely refers to some concerned friends who believed that Jesus could heal their blind friend. This miracle represents Jesus' response to the faith of these friends and probably the faith of the blind man. Many of the healing miracles are tied to faith, but not all of them. Jesus

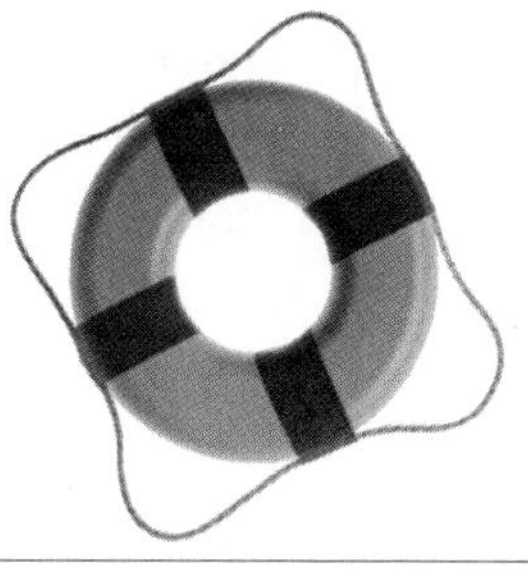

initiated the contact with the man born blind in John 9, but in this case friends took the initiative. Faith is often the trigger that releases the power of the Savior.

This display of the Savior's power raises some interesting questions. First, *Why did Jesus take the blind man by the hand and lead him out of the village?* Some blame it on Bethsaida since Jesus had earlier pronounced judgment on this village because they had rejected the light they had received through His ministry (Matt. 11:21-22). However, it may simply be that Jesus did not want any more publicity. Jesus never used His power to call attention to Himself. Rather, His miracles were an expression of the power of God and a confirmation of the reality of the kingdom.

Another question might be, *Why did Jesus spit on his eyes?* "Spitting on his eyes and laying His hands on him, He asked him, 'Do you see anything?'" (Mark 8:23). There was no healing power in the spittle, but it was rather an encouragement to the faith of the blind man. It helped the man focus on his need and the readiness of Jesus to heal him. In this case Jesus also laid hands on the man. Jesus' method was always related to the need of the individual. The means did not enhance His power—He was able to do whatever He willed to do at any time.

A CLOSER LOOK

Mark 8:22-26

"Perhaps Mark recorded the story to show that the messianic age as prophesied by Isaiah (e.g., 19:18; 35:5) was present in Jesus. Very important is the symbolism of the two-stage healing. The disciples, like the blind man, had been 'touched' by Jesus and had received a preliminary blessing. Their spiritual insight, however, was far from complete. It was not much better than that of the Pharisees. They needed a 'second touch' for complete understanding."

James A. Brooks, *Mark* in *The New American Commentary,* vol. 23 (Nashville: Broadman Press, 1994), 133.

A more serious question could be, *Why was the miracle gradual?* After the application of the spittle, the man had some sight. He said, "I see people—they look to me like trees walking" (v. 24). Since he could recognize trees and persons, he probably was not born blind. He remembered what trees looked like when he still had sight, but his sight was not fully restored.

After Jesus placed His hands on him a second time, "he saw distinctly. He was cured and could see everything clearly" (v. 25). Is there a lesson to be learned by this gradual healing, especially since the Holy Spirit placed it in this particular context? Some scholars believe that there is. They see the disciples as being much like the blind man because though Jesus had touched them, they did not see things clearly. If they were to see things clearly, it would require a second touch. Some relate this second touch to the things that would happen in the immediate future, while others relate it to Pentecost and the promised baptism in the Holy Spirit. Clearly, the disciples were in a state of confusion right up to the day that the ascended Lord sent the Holy Spirit to indwell them.

There is no question about the basic lesson of the miracle. Jesus has the power to finish what He has begun. He would not leave this man half-healed. And He has the power to help us! He will not leave us in our confusion and uncertainty. He has the power to bring us to the point that we can see things clearly. As long as we are in this world, we will continue to see "indistinctly, as in a mirror"; but before He is through, we will see "face to face" (1 Cor. 13:12).

Good news! Not only can Jesus help you, but He will help you. His arms are always open to those the religious world has shut out, to those struggling with their attempts to believe, and to those who will admit their blindness. The only ones He cannot help are those who continue to deny that they need His help. Jesus' help is only a prayer away.

your notes

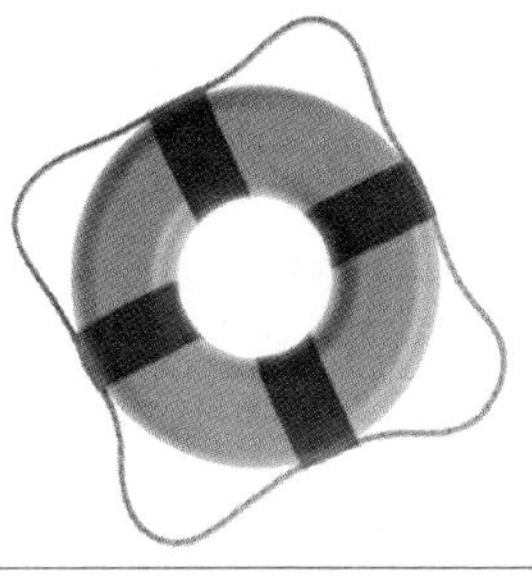

Session 3

How Can I Be More Consistent?

Scripture **Mark 8:27–10:52**
Focal: Mark 8:27–38; 9:14–29,33–37; 10:35–45

During my 50 years of Christian ministry, Billy Graham has been one of my heroes. As a teenage pastor in the mountains of Tennessee, I would listen with awe to his radio program "The Hour of Decision." Dr. Graham was already proclaiming Christ to millions and on his way to doing so on a global scale.

Along with his effectiveness, Dr. Graham's consistency has been the thing I have admired most. Even though the world has been in turmoil throughout his ministry, he has been faithful to proclaim the truth of the gospel and to model it in his life. He has been above reproach in his conduct. In this he has been like our Lord who lived the ultimate life of consistency.

The first disciples were like us—they struggled for consistency. They could move so quickly from victory to shame. In the paragraphs we are studying, Peter gave his great confession only to reveal that he did not understand the necessity of the cross. The disciples could move from victory to victory in ministry only to be totally frustrated by a stubborn demon. James and John could move from the privilege of the transfiguration experience to starting a conflict over who would be first in the kingdom. If we listen to the Teacher as He dealt with these inconsistencies, we can learn about living a consistent life of discipleship. Having read extensively about the life and ministry of

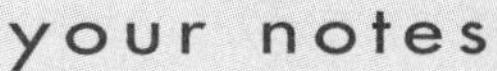

Dr. Graham, I am convinced that he learned the secret of consistency from Jesus.

EMBRACE THE CROSS (MARK 8:27-38)

The question at Caesarea Philippi marked a turning point in the life of Jesus. From this point on, His face would be turned toward the end in Jerusalem. So He tested the disciples. Did they know who He was? Were they ready to embrace the cross, which was an absolute necessity for His role as Messiah?

For Your Consideration

1. How would you answer the question concerning the identity of Jesus?

2. Why was it necessary for Jesus to "suffer many things"?

3. Why did Peter rebuke Jesus?

4. How does a person deny himself or herself?

5. How is the disciple's cross different from the cross of Christ?

6. What does it mean to lose one's life for Jesus' sake?

As He set His face toward the cross, Jesus asked *the* question: "But you, . . . who do you say that I am?" (v. 29). They had already given a report on what others were saying about Him. The common people were identifying Him as John the Baptist, Elijah, or one of the prophets. But "you [the disciples as a group], who do you say that I am?" It was their turn to answer this critical question. No one will ever face a more important question. Where you spend eternity depends on your knowing the answer to this question.

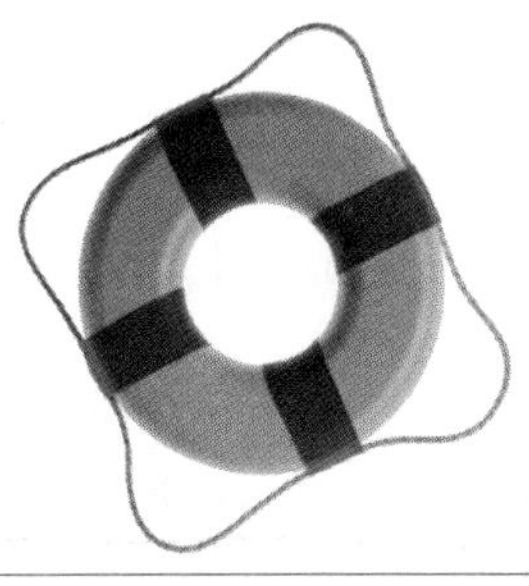

Peter answered for the group, "You are the Messiah!" (v. 29). This confession related Jesus to the promises in the Old Testament and the hopes of the nation of Israel. For generations the nation had been waiting for the Messiah to come and restore the nation to the glory it had known under King David. The disciples were convinced that He was this Messiah, which means "the anointed one."

Jesus accepted the confession of Peter as true but "strictly warned them to tell no one about Him" (v. 30). He knew that what Israel expected from their Messiah and the mission that He had been given by the Father were in conflict with each other. To broadcast Jesus' claim to be the Messiah could ignite uncontrollable political excitement.

The disciples needed to know the truth about Jesus' mission, so "He began to teach them that the Son of Man must suffer many things" (v. 31). The leaders of the nation would reject His messianic claims and have Him killed, but He would rise after three days. Never were the disciples more shocked! Peter found a private moment with Jesus "to rebuke Him" (v. 32). Rejection and death were not in their plans. Jesus must forget such ideas. He is the Messiah! They had failed to include the Suffering Servant prophecy (Isa. 52:13–53:12) in their expectations.

Then it was Peter's turn to hear a stern word of rebuke: "Get behind Me, Satan, because you're not thinking about God's concerns, but man's!" (Mark 8:33). Peter was offering Jesus the same counsel Satan gave Him in the wilderness (see Matt. 4:8-10)—to be a Messiah without a cross. A suffering Messiah was not man's idea but God's.

We must be prepared to embrace the cross of Christ. Jesus came to be the Suffering Son of Man. It was the will of His Heavenly Father that He suffer and then be exalted and crowned. The "must" of His sufferings reveals the nature of His redemptive mission as well as the depth of human sinfulness. Are you prepared to follow the Son of Man who surrendered to suffering and death for you?

When you chose to follow Jesus, you chose to follow the Suffering Savior. The Suffering Savior leads people who are prepared to suffer with Him and for Him.

Actually Jesus spoke the words about the disciple's cross to "the crowd along with His disciples" (Mark 8:34). His words were very clear and direct: "he must deny himself" (v. 34). Self can no longer be the center of one's life; Jesus must be the center. What the self wants can no longer be a priority; the first priority is what Jesus wants.

A CLOSER LOOK

Who Is Jesus?

Just a myth
Or perhaps a legend
Maybe a miracle worker
A visionary
A revolutionary
A brilliant religious teacher and leader
A great prophet—possibly the greatest of them all
An angel

Most of these views about Jesus are incorrect, and all of them are woefully inadequate. The Scriptures teach that Jesus is much more. He is the Messiah— the "Anointed One"—and the Son of God sent by the Father to redeem sinful humanity. Salvation comes to a person only by faith in Jesus, the One who died for our sins.

your notes

After denying self, a person must "take up his cross, and follow Me" (v. 34). Condemned criminals were required to carry the crossbeam through the streets to the place of execution. By this public act they were subjected to the scorn of the crowd and forced to submit to the authority of Rome. Jesus would do this very thing before His own execution. Does this mean that if I follow Jesus I will die a shameful death? It may; it may not. But it really doesn't matter. The main issue in life must be following Jesus—not preserving my life or finding pleasure for myself. We must be prepared to do the will of God regardless of the cost.

Jesus attached a series of warnings to this statement, each beginning with "for." These warnings tell us that

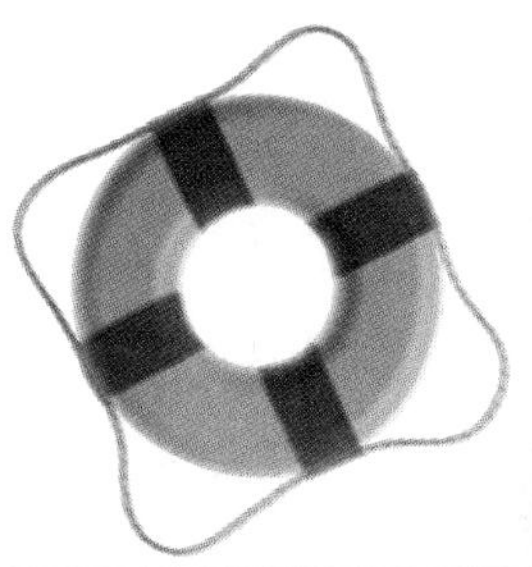

Learning Activity

Tracking Peter's Responses

Answer the following questions about Peter's interaction with Jesus. The evaluation will shed some light on the value of consistency in following Christ.

Mark 8:29

What did Peter say about Jesus?

What did Peter's confession imply about his devotion to Christ?

Mark 8:32

Why did Peter rebuke Jesus?

What did Peter's rebuke of Jesus imply about his devotion to Christ?

Mark 8:33

Why did Jesus rebuke Peter?

What did Jesus' rebuke suggest about being consistent in following Him?

the only life worth living is found through giving up your life in submission and obedience to the Son of Man (vv. 35-38). Those who put Him first in everything find fullness of life now and in eternity. Those who pursue a selfish agenda lose everything in the end. The only authentic life known to Jesus begins with embracing the cross—His and yours.

Grow in Faith (Mark 9:14-29)

Faith is essential to the consistent life. Jesus seized every opportunity to encourage faith in His followers. Their embarrassing failure to cast out the demon from the troubled child made them open to a new lesson on faith. The lesson is simple: in life and in service, faith is everything. Do we dare allow the Lord to show us how and why we have failed?

For Your Consideration

1. Why did the disciples fail to deliver the boy from the demon?

2. Is it appropriate to pray for greater faith? Why or why not?

3. Is a failure to get a miracle when we pray always a failure of faith? Why or why not?

4. What is the relationship between prayer and faith?

5. What is the relationship between prayer and fasting?

Jesus used Peter's painful moment of failure to encourage His disciples with the potential of faith. It happened after Jesus had been on the mount of transfiguration with Peter, James, and John (9:1-13). After they had descended from the mount, Jesus found the other nine disciples engaged in a debate with the

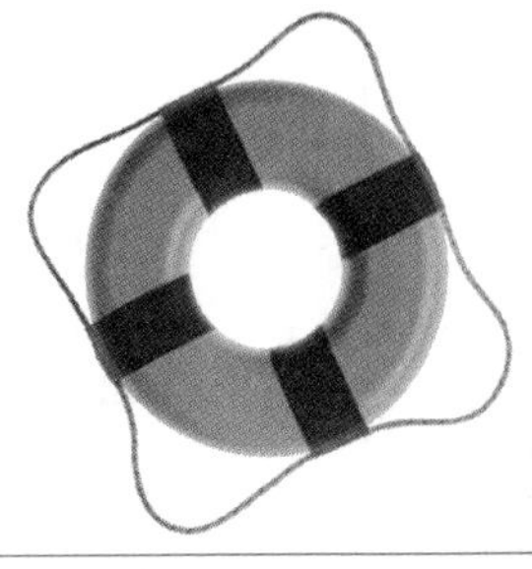

scribes. When Jesus inquired about the nature of the debate, a distraught father blurted out the failure of His disciples. The man had brought his demon-possessed son to the disciples for deliverance, but they failed in their attempts to help the boy.

While the description of the child's condition sounds like modern epilepsy, Jesus treated this as a case of demon possession. This does not mean that there is a connection between demon possession and epilepsy. The only similarity is in some of the symptoms. One is a medical condition and the other is a spiritual condition.

Jesus immediately identified the cause for the failure: "O, unbelieving generation! How long will I be with you: How long must I put up with you?" (Mark 9:19). The father and the disciples were still part of the unbelieving generation like the scribes. Where there is unbelief, there is no power.

As Jesus continued the conversation with the father, He received a firsthand report on the condition of the boy. The father stated in desperation, "But if You can do anything, have compassion on us and help us" (v. 22). The "if" triggered a response from Jesus—"'If You can?'" Everything is possible to the one who believes" (v. 23). This states the potential of faith—"Everything is possible"! Jesus was both challenging the father to become a person of faith and presenting Himself as the example of faith. Never forget the humanity of Jesus. He too walked and lived by faith.

Jesus then demonstrated the potential of faith by restoring the troubled child to wholeness. As a man of powerful faith, Jesus commanded the demons to come out of the boy and they obeyed. Even though the experience left the boy physically and emotionally drained, he was free

A CLOSER LOOK

Faith and Prayer

Faith is not changing the will of God. Rather, it is being close enough to God to know His will and to ask for what He wills to do. This does not place limits on prayer. God is always ready to do more than we ask (see Eph. 3:20; 1 John 5:14-15).

your notes

from this evil presence in his life. Wherever there is faith, all things are possible!

The response of the father to the word about the potential of faith points in the right direction. He "cried out, 'I do believe! Help my unbelief'" (v. 24). To become strong in faith, we need the help of the Lord. Earnest prayer for stronger faith is in order.

Afterwards, however, the disciples were shown the path to faith. They asked Jesus privately about their powerlessness over the demons. Jesus responded, "This kind can come out by nothing but prayer [and fasting]" (v. 29). He was clearly making a connection between their lack of faith and prayerlessness. Had they acted presumptuously? Had casting out demons become so routine that they had forgotten that it was God's work, not theirs?

This puts things in a new light. Jesus was able to act in faith because His faith was renewed in His time of communion with the Father. Luke reported that the transfiguration happened while Jesus was praying (Luke 9:29). If the words "and fasting" are considered part of the text (as in the HCSB), then remember that fasting enables one to devote more thought and energy to prayer. An effective prayer life will produce greater faith. This is the key to Christlike consistency in life.

Develop a Servant Lifestyle (Mark 9:33-37; 10:35-45)

While Jesus was sharing with them the sobering words about His suffering (9:30-32), the disciples were involved in a conflict over who would be first in His kingdom. How out of step with the Teacher could they be? Jesus waited for a private moment in the house in Capernaum to settle their argument. He wanted them to have a place of honor in His kingdom, but honor is given to those who have a servant lifestyle.

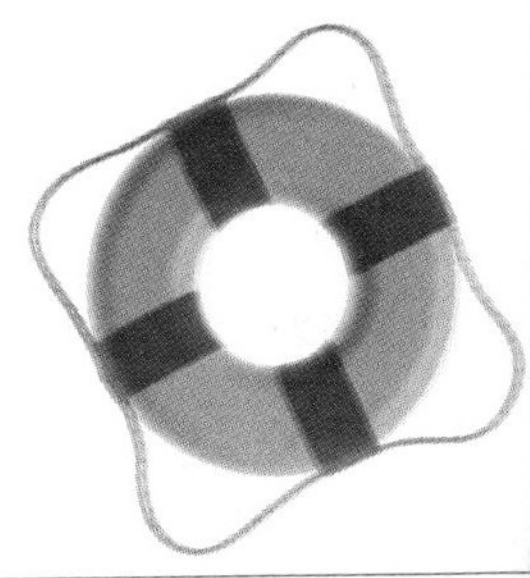

Learning Activity

Consistency Checkup

Evaluate your level of consistency as a disciple of Jesus Christ. Use a scale of 1 (very inconsistent) to 10 (very consistent) and rate yourself on each of the following issues. A perfect score is 100.

___ 1. I affirm that Jesus is the Messiah.

___ 2. I am growing in my understanding of what the cross of Christ means.

___ 3. I am willing every day to deny myself, take up my cross, and follow Jesus.

___ 4. I am willing to submit myself to the Lord and sacrifice myself for the sake of others.

___ 5. I have faith in Christ that makes me call on Him for help.

___ 6. I spend some time every day in prayer.

___ 7. I want to grow in my faith in Christ.

___ 8. I am devoted to a lifestyle of serving as opposed to being served.

___ 9. I try to serve the people whom others consider to be insignificant.

___10. I consistently ask Jesus to help me grow as a disciple devoted to serving.

What's your score? _____ What do you intend to do to improve it?

For Your Consideration

1. Does Jesus approve or disapprove of spiritual ambition in His statement about servanthood? Why?

2. Do you have a servant's spirit? If not, what can you do to develop one in your life?

3. What is the relationship between denying self and being a servant of all?

4. Have you ever seen selfish ambition cause division in a church? How could it have been stopped?

5. What does it mean to welcome one as a little child?

6. What is the reward for welcoming a child?

7. Is this statement limited to just young children or does it apply to any weak person?

Jesus took the customary position of a Jewish teacher for this lesson: "Sitting down, He called the Twelve" (v. 35). Then He shared a first principle in His kingdom: "If anyone wants to be first, he must be last of all and servant of all" (v. 35). While Jesus would commend the aspiration to be first in His kingdom, the person must know that His kingdom is different. In this world a person's greatness is measured by how many people serve that person, but in the kingdom of God it is measured by how many people a person serves.

The Greek word for "servant" does not mean "slave" but rather "one who serves another." The word is translated "deacon" in other places. The attitude of the servant is one of humility. Such an attitude values others above self and considers it a privilege to meet the needs of other people. Paul explained that this mind-set or attitude is best seen in Jesus (Phil. 2:4-11).

your notes

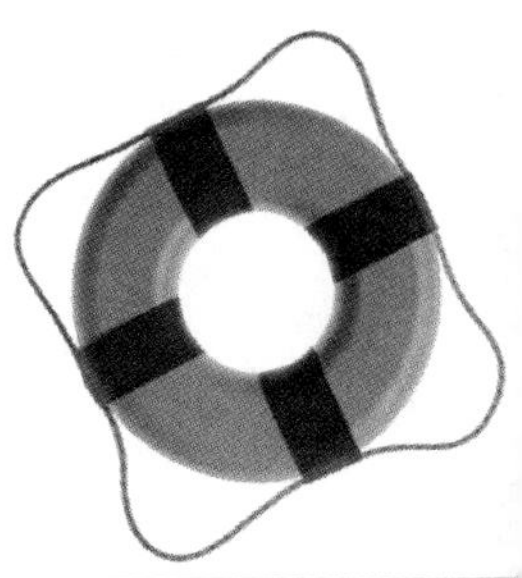

As a visual aid for the point He was making, Jesus "took a child" and "had him stand among them" (Mark 9:36). He then took the child "in His arms" to demonstrate how the servant attitude works. If they were actually in the home of Peter in Capernaum, the child could have been one of his children. The attitude of the Roman and (to a degree) Jewish culture toward children is that they had no status. They exercised no influence. Their position in the home was on the same level as a servant. So Jesus' words gave them something new to consider in relation to God's kingdom.

Jesus explained, "Whoever welcomes one little child such as this in My name welcomes Me" (v. 37). To welcome is to receive with gladness, to treat as a person of worth, to serve. To welcome is to be concerned about someone's welfare. To welcome the child "in My name" is to do so as Christ's representative—which is the way a Christian should do everything.

Jesus encouraged such actions by the promise He attached to it: "And whoever welcomes Me does not welcome Me, but Him who sent Me" (v. 37). When you serve a little one—such as a person that the world looks down on—you serve Jesus. When you serve Jesus, you actually serve the Eternal Father who sent Jesus. The clear implication is that those who receive the Son and the Father by serving the weak and helpless will be the ones honored in the kingdom.

If this is true, why is it so difficult to get adults to work with preschoolers and children in the contemporary church? These words of Jesus make even more sense when we consider what modern studies have revealed about the importance of the early years in a person's development. Someone who serves a child may contribute more to the work of the kingdom than someone who administers a large program or chairs an important committee.

Those who know my hero Billy Graham best are impressed with his genuine humility. His life and ministry amaze me, but he has always seen himself as a servant. So the way to consistency is clear—embrace the cross, grow in faith, and develop a servant's lifestyle. Such a consistent life blesses you and others both now and in eternity.

Session 3

CHAPTER 6

What If Others Don't Believe?

Scripture **Mark 11:1–12:44**
Focal: Mark 11:12–12:12

William Carey persevered in Christian service to the end of his life. He believed that the gospel of Christ must be shared with everyone. It was a revolutionary idea among the evangelical Christians of his generation, and most of them rejected it. His own wife reluctantly joined him in the pursuit of his calling. He slipped into India illegally because the normal channels were closed. When he arrived, he faced one disappointment after another. He found a culture that was not open to the message that he brought.

Financial hardships, sickness, betrayal, and the danger of death were some of the situations Carey endured, but he never turned back. He never returned to England—not even for a vacation—but died in the country to which God had sent him. Carey serves as a reminder to us that every believer has an assignment from God, even if others don't agree. This was a way of life that Jesus demonstrated and taught others to follow. Carey has been honored with the title "The Father of Modern Missions" for his faithfulness. Jesus wears the title "Lord and Savior." How will we respond to a culture that is addicted to unbelief?

Learn to Be Obedient (Mark 11:12-21)

Jerusalem was in a buzz! Jesus had stirred the city with His dramatic entrance on Sunday (Mark 11:1-11). While a small company was ready to receive Him as Messiah, the elite of Judaism remained adamant in their opposition. They wanted Him dead, and the sooner the better. It was in this charged atmosphere that Jesus gave two dramatic parables. The lesson for a believer in Jesus is clear: Regardless of what others do, obey the Lord!

For Your Consideration

1. What is the significance of the "leaves" in this report?

2. What is the fruit God desires?

3. What are the dangers of making the practice of our faith convenient?

4. What would Jesus change about your church if He came for a visit?

5. What was Jesus' attitude as He cleansed the temple? Was He angry or grieved or both?

The details of the fig tree incident are rather clear, but many wonder what Jesus' purpose was in cursing the tree. It was Monday morning, and Jesus was on His way back into Jerusalem after spending the night in Bethany. He was hungry and saw a fig tree covered with leaves. Even though it was not the season for a tree to have figs, it normally put on fruit before it put on leaves. The leaves advertised fruit, but upon inspection Jesus found nothing but leaves. Obviously this tree would not bear fruit that year so Jesus declared, "May no one ever eat fruit from you again!" (v. 14). As they returned to Jerusalem the next day, they discovered that the tree was completely withered (v. 20) and Peter called attention to it (v. 21).

This miracle was likely an enacted parable by Jesus—a miracle with a self-contained message. A tree represents the nation of Israel many times in the Old Testament, just as the fig tree does here. Jesus came to the nation looking for fruit but found none. All of the outward signs of religion were present (leaves), but there was no faith, love, or obedience to God (fruit). Fruitfulness is experienced as we relate to God in love and obedience. This is a lesson for religious people in every age.

Jesus inspected the temple carefully on Sunday (v. 11) but did not respond to what He saw. He waited until Monday. Then in another enacted parable He expressed His holy displeasure with what He saw: "He

your notes

Learning Activity

Facing Unbelief

Mark 11:12–12:12 addresses the difficult truth that many people will refuse to believe in Jesus Christ. Answer the following questions with this difficult truth in mind.

1. How can I learn to be obedient on a consistent basis?

2. How can I experience the power of faith in my daily walk with God?

3. In what ways will knowing the fallacies of unbelief increase my faith?

4. In what ways will understanding the nature of unbelief increase my faith?

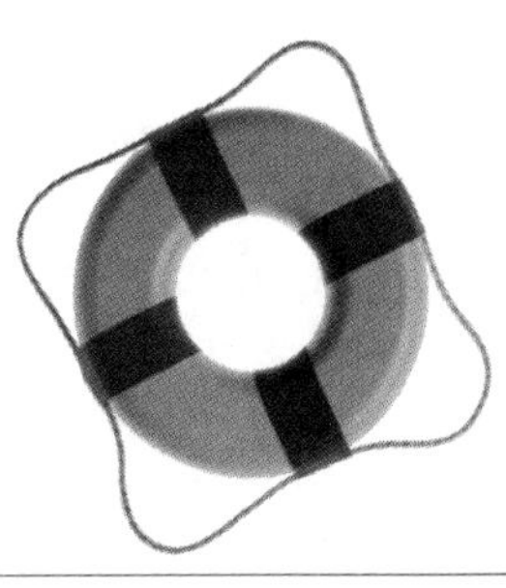

overturned the money changers' tables and the chairs of those selling doves, and would not permit anyone to carry goods through the temple complex" (vv. 15-16). Under the guise of making worship easier for the people, the religious rulers had set up a little market in the court of the Gentiles. There someone could exchange secular coins for the sacred coins required for paying the temple tax or purchasing an appropriate bird or animal for sacrifice. This convenience likely cost more than it should have and was something everyone had to follow, so it enriched those who operated the market.

The people had also made a common passageway out of the court of the Gentiles. It saved time to walk through the temple rather than to take the longer way around the temple mount.

After Jesus had taken the corrective steps, He justified His actions by quoting from two of the most respected Jewish prophets, Isaiah and Jeremiah. Isaiah quoted God as declaring that the temple was to be "a house of prayer for all nations" (v. 17; see Isa. 56:7). The religious leaders had essentially severed the Gentiles' access to the temple by taking for their use the one court the Gentiles could enter to pray. Jeremiah had accused the leaders of using the temple as a place to hide, "a den of thieves" (v. 17; see Jer. 7:11). The corrupt leaders were attempting to hide their spiritual barrenness and corruption under the activities performed in the temple, and Jesus judged them for it. Before the week was over, Jesus would predict the complete destruction of this beautiful temple (Mark 13:1-2). The failure of the leaders and thus the nation to receive Him as their Messiah and Lord would result in judgment.

We must not miss the lesson: Fruitfulness is important and grows out of obedience. This hard truth will never change. Cheap and corrupt religious practices are offensive to the Lord of the church.

Consider the Power of Faith (Mark 11:22-26)

Jesus explained the plight of the tree. All of Jesus' works—including the cursing of the tree—were done by faith. He did not explain the significance of the cursing, for it must have been obvious to the disciples in that context. They must have surmised that Jesus was giving a lesson on Israel and the temple. But He got their eyes off the temple and the nation and on to their personal faith.

your notes

For Your Consideration

1. How would you define the word *faith*?

2. Who else or what else do people have as objects of faith other than God?

3. What mountains does your church face in its ministry?

4. How do you reconcile this passage with our unanswered prayers?

5. Are the unforgiving always unforgiven? Why?

Jesus' statement pointed the disciples to the object of their faith: "Have faith in God" (v. 22). The disciples had to continue to trust in and rely on God regardless of the fate of the temple and the nation. This was not easy for these Jewish men. The temple and the nation had always been a part of their religious lives. What would life be like without them? They had to discover that the real object of faith will always be there and that He does not change. He will never be less than adequate as an object of their faith.

A CLOSER LOOK

Prayer and Faith

"When prayer is the source of faith's power and the means of its strength, God's sovereignty is its only restriction."

William L. Lane, *The Gospel According to Mark* (Grand Rapids: Eerdmans, 1974), 410.

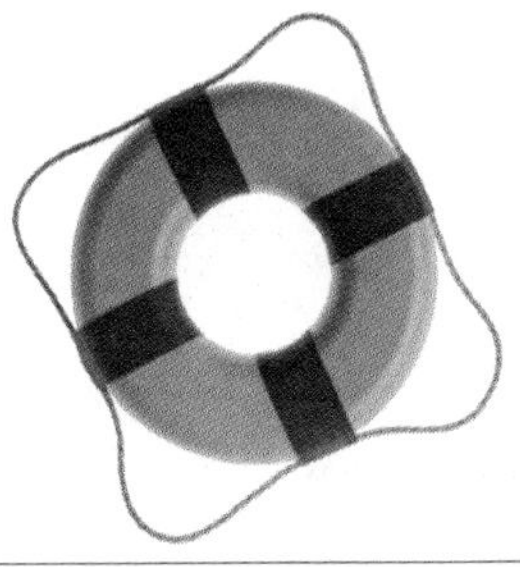

Learning Activity

Making Inspections

Mark 11 describes Jesus' inspection of the temple. Use the text as a guide and write down the standard He used in His inspection. Compare it to the standard that seemed to be used by the religious leaders who opposed Him.

The Standard of Worship (Mark 11:15-18)

According to Jesus

According to the religious leaders

The Standard of Faith (Mark 11:27-33)

According to Jesus

According to the religious leaders

your notes

Suppose the support system for your faith was removed. Could you make it without your family? your church? While the institutions of family and church have important roles in our lives, the living God is the true object of our faith. He will always be there.

After the command to maintain faith, Jesus gave the promise: "I assure you: If anyone says to this mountain, 'Be lifted up and thrown into the sea,' and does not doubt in his heart, but believes that what he says will happen, it will be done for him" (v. 23). What is "this mountain"? Jewish teachers used such an image to speak of overcoming obstacles. This is the best way to understand Jesus' statement. It is not so much about performing a miracle as it is about overcoming by faith what appears to be an insurmountable obstacle.

These disciples would need this promise. As they undertook the mission Jesus gave them—taking the gospel to the whole world—they would face many obstacles, some human and some not. However, they should "speak" only of the accomplishment of the task. What God assigns He enables.

We must not discount the importance of words in expressing faith. While some have pushed the truth about words of faith to ridiculous extremes, the reality must not be lost. Our words do express our faith—and our doubts.

Prayer can also be an expression of faith. "Therefore, I tell you, all the things you pray and ask for—believe that you have received them, and you will have them" (v. 24). While we must be cautious about extending this statement to every human situation, we must understand that faith is always an important element in prayer. Faith will not override the will of God, but rather true faith will desire the will of God above everything else. True faith will rejoice in the will of the Heavenly Father, even when it conflicts with our deepest desires (Mark 14:36; see 1 John 5:14).

Why did Jesus then discuss forgiveness? Actually it is not unusual for Jesus to connect prayer with forgiving

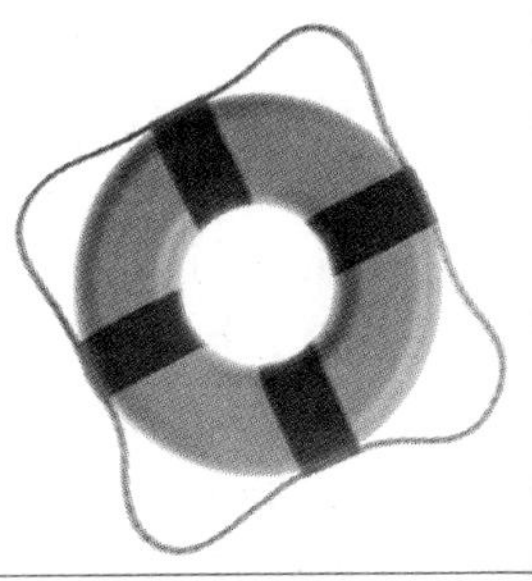

others (see Matt. 6:14-15). An unforgiving spirit hinders a person from really experiencing God's best and limits the power of prayer. It stunts our faith when we are standing before God in prayer.

While it helps to have others stand with you in faith, if they refuse, keep the faith as Caleb and Joshua did (Num. 13:26-33). Declare your confidence in the Lord. In the end God will vindicate your faith. These two men were the only survivors from a doomed generation, but they persevered by faith to enter the promised land.

Observe the Fallacies of Unbelief (Mark 11:27-33)

Unbelief is ugly, especially when it dresses in the cloaks of religion. Jesus provoked expressions of unbelief by His bold action in the temple. There were numerous attempts to ensnare or embarrass Him during these lasts days of His life (11:27–12:44). The Jewish leaders were actively looking for a rationale for putting Him to death. Lest we fall into unbelief, we need to understand the nature of unbelief.

For Your Consideration

1. Why did the Jewish leaders refuse to believe in Jesus as their Messiah?

2. What have you heard others say to justify their unbelief?

3. How do you respond to a person who is verbally justifying his or her unbelief?

4. How did you justify your own unbelief before you were saved?

During that last week of Jesus' life, public appearances attracted the Jewish leaders and others speaking on their behalf. On this occasion, "the chief priests, the scribes, and the elders" demanded credentials from Him: "By what authority are You doing these things? Who gave You this authority to do these things?" (11:27-28). "These things" refers to the cleansing of the temple. They were the official keepers of the temple, and they had not given Him authority to act in this manner.

Jesus was so wise in dealing with His critics! He presented a question to them as a condition for answering their question: "Was John's baptism

your notes

from heaven or from men?" (v. 30). It was known that John the Baptist had identified Jesus as "the Lamb of God" and had confessed Jesus to be greater than himself (see John 1:32-35). Yet these officials had not accepted John and his witness about Jesus' identity. Whichever way they answered the question, they were trapped. The masses would not forgive them if they denied the validity of John's ministry, but if it was from heaven, why were they not accepting His witness concerning Jesus?

In an attempt to save face, these leaders backed off and declined to give an answer, and Jesus refused to answer them as well (Mark 11:31-33). They decided to wait for another opportunity to trap Him. Their whole agenda was to justify their unbelief. They were not looking for a reason to receive Him, but for a reason to justify killing Him. This is the nature of unbelief.

Understand the Nature of Unbelief (Mark 12:1-12)

Surely no one missed the punch line in the parable of the vineyard. The vineyard was a familiar image for the nation of Israel. God was described as the Owner and Keeper of the vineyard (Isa. 5). The servants who received abusive and deadly treatment would be the prophets. But "he still had one to send, a beloved son. Finally he sent him to them, saying, 'They will respect my son' " (Mark 12:6), and they understood that Jesus was referring to Himself.

For Your Consideration

1. Would you agree that the sending of the beloved son was an extreme measure by the owner? Why?

2. Do you see evidence of such unbelief in our culture? Where is it most evident?

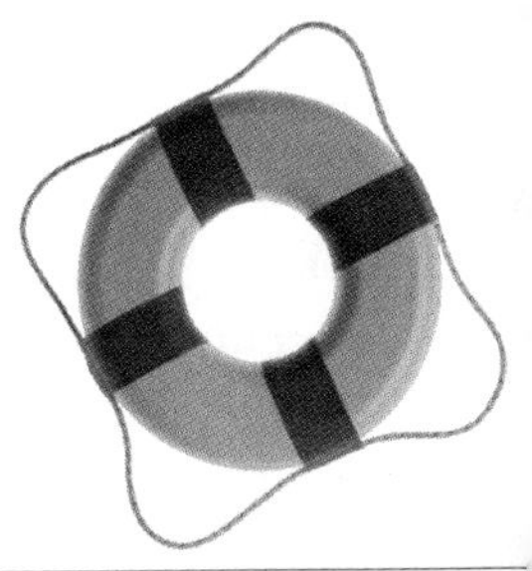

3. How might we rob God of His glory today?

4. What rights does God have over us simply because He is God?

5. What application does this story have to a local church? to a denomination?

6. What are the consequences to the individual who persists in unbelief?

This story so graphically matches what actually happened that some have claimed it was created after the fact. But it is obvious from His many statements about His impending death that Jesus understood it perfectly. It is better to accept this revealing truth: Unbelief totally rejected Jesus and even put Him to death when the opportunity arose. This stands in contrast to faith that receives Him and confesses Him as Lord. This should warn us that it could be dangerous to live in times when unbelief prevails.

So what did the farmers in the parable do? "They seized him [the son] and killed him, and threw him out of the vineyard" (v. 8). This is the ultimate act of unbelief!

Obviously the owner had a right to the income from his vineyard. No one would deny that his expectation was just. But the wicked tenants wanted his property for themselves. They refused to relate to the owner as the owner. But in our understanding of the parable, what does the income from the vineyard represent? We know that the owner represents the God of Israel, so what was He expecting from His vineyard? Was it not glory and honor? Did He not expect the Israelites to relate to Him as the God of the covenant and to love Him with their total beings (vv. 28-34)? Unbelief puts self at the center of life and refuses to give God what is rightfully His.

Jesus left no doubt about the outcome of unbelief. The owner of the vineyard will not allow this kind of behavior to go unpunished. The wicked tenants must pay for their treatment of his son. They would be destroyed and the vineyard given to others. Jesus quoted an Old Testament prophecy to support His application of this story to Israel. In the prophecy the rejected stone becomes the cornerstone.

The outcome of Israel's unbelief is a matter of history. In A.D. 70 Israel lost its temple, its capital city, and its statehood. The God of the covenant raised up a new people, made up of Jews and Gentiles, through which to

your notes

A CLOSER LOOK

William Carey

William Carey was born in England in 1761. He trusted Christ at the age of 18 and began serving as a pastor seven years later. Carey became convinced that Christians need to preach the gospel to everyone, so he founded the Baptist Missionary Society in 1792. The next year Carey and his family sailed for India where he served as a missionary in the region of Bengal until his death in 1834.

do His work (see Eph. 3:5-7). But this new people, the church, must be a people of faith or they will suffer the fate of Israel (Rom. 11:20-21).

This story is not addressing directly the question of the salvation of the individual but rather the fate of people who are full of unbelief. The Jews did not lose their religion; they lost their faith. They still had the forms, but no substance. Paul warned of a generation of Christians who would have the "form of religion," but they would deny "its power" (2 Tim. 3:5). His counsel was to avoid such people.

What do you do when others do not believe? Keep growing in your faith. Avoid unbelief at all cost. Remember people like William Carey who were faithful to the end.

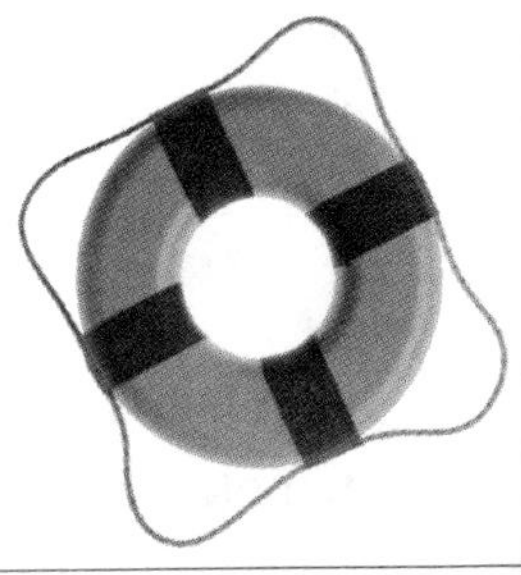

Session 4

What About the Future?

Scripture **Mark 13:1–37**
Focal: Mark 13:5–37

Some people turn to psychics when they have questions about the future. This can be a dangerous practice. When four psychics opened the Manitou Centre of Light and Healing, they promised a money back guarantee if their predictions were not accurate. But when their new building burned four months later, with no fire insurance, Alison Neves, one of the partners said, "The spirits we work with don't always know what is going to happen." True! Since the source of information of true psychics is often demonic, their spirits know nothing for sure about the future.

Jesus was the Prophet of prophets, not a psychic. His Heavenly Father, who knows all things, was His source concerning the future (John 14:10). If you have questions about the future, listen to the Lord Jesus! His Source knows all things—past, present, and future. Jesus gave trustworthy guidance with reference to the future. He provided just enough information about the future to comfort us, to encourage us to be faithful, and to finish the tasks He has given us.

Recognize Deceivers (Mark 13:5-8)

When the disciples raised questions about the destruction of the temple and the end of the age, Jesus told them about future events just

your notes

prior to His return. Since Jesus has not yet returned, these words are for us as well as for the first disciples. We need to be aware of the distractions that will keep us from focusing on what is really important.

For Your Consideration

1. Can you name some prominent deceivers who have appeared in the last 50 years?

2. How do you explain the success of such deceivers?

3. What can you do to protect yourself from the false teachers?

4. Why has every generation been filled with wars and rumors of wars?

5. If these future things are "birth pains," what is about to be born?

False messiahs and false prophets are always a threat. Jesus said that in the end times such men would come making false claims: "Many will come in My name, saying, 'I am He,' and they will deceive many" (v. 6). "In My name" indicates they claim either to be the Messiah (Christ) or to represent Him.

Jesus was right! Many have come in the generations since He spoke these words, and they have deceived many. The government trains its agents to detect counterfeit money by making them so acquainted with genuine bills that they can detect the false immediately. We must know Christ and the gospel of His salvation so well that we can easily recognize the false. We must not allow charlatans to distract us from our main task of taking the true gospel to all nations.

Troublesome times can also be a distraction, so Jesus warned, "don't be alarmed!" The reports "of wars and rumors of wars" (v. 7), conflicts between

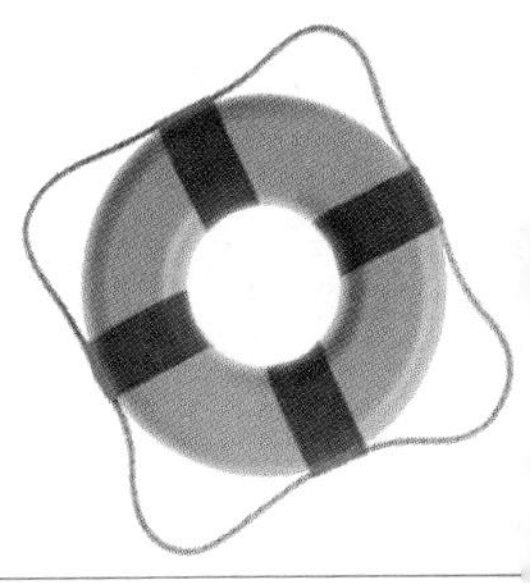

Learning Activity

Be on Guard

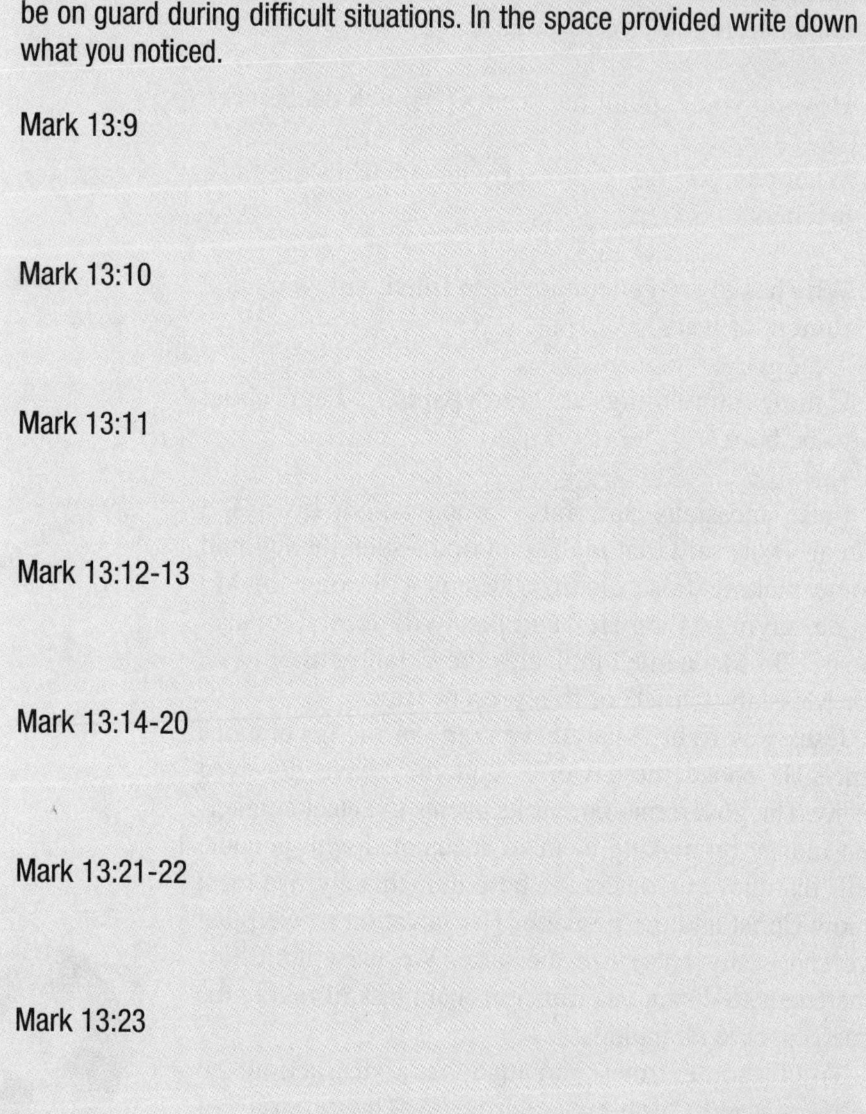

Glean from the following passages of Scripture the ways in which you can be on guard during difficult situations. In the space provided write down what you noticed.

Mark 13:9

Mark 13:10

Mark 13:11

Mark 13:12-13

Mark 13:14-20

Mark 13:21-22

Mark 13:23

your notes

nations, earthquakes, and famines do not mean that the end is immediately near. Rather they are just the beginning of the birth pains that will culminate in the coming of the King. Followers of Jesus are to understand that such is normal for a fallen world and keep focused on the assignment they have been given to take the gospel to all the tribes of the earth. Recognize them for what they are—a source of alarm indicating that the end is not yet here but is close at hand.

Be on Guard for Difficulties (Mark 13:9-23)

Jesus predicted that His people would do their work in a hostile and dangerous environment. God's people need to be prepared for such situations and determine ahead of time that they will remain faithful to Christ and the gospel.

For Your Consideration

1. How much of the persecution of Christians is provoked by their attempts to share the gospel with the whole world?

2. How are the sufferings of Christians at the hands of the world different from the sufferings of Jesus? How are they the same?

3. Why is enduring to the end not a condition of salvation but evidence of saving faith?

4. What should our response be to the persecution of other Christians?

5. Define "tribulation" as Jesus used it. What would a tribulation be in our day?

6. When would it be wrong to flee a dangerous situation? When would it be appropriate?

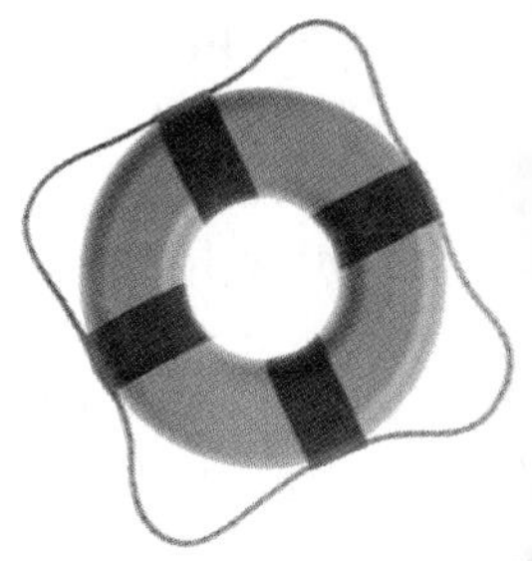

7. What does it mean to be "the elect" (v. 20)?

The propagation of the gospel to all nations provoked persecution in the first century and continues to provoke it. There is a similarity in language describing what happened to the disciples and what happened to Jesus. Both were handed over, flogged, arrested, and hated. Jesus' sufferings were a sacrifice for our sins, and disciples are a witness to His name and gospel.

While this passage does caution us about danger in such difficulties, it also provides encouragement. We will be enabled to speak a word of witness by the Holy Spirit (v. 11), and our faith in Christ will be confirmed by our steadfastness under such pressure (v. 13). The most severe form of persecution comes when those we love turn against us and join others in calling for our death. All indications are that the 21st century is going to be marked by severe persecution and many deaths for the cause of Christ. We must not allow persecution to discourage us. These words prepared Peter and John to rejoice when they were flogged for preaching the gospel (Acts 5:40-42). Instead of seeking a place of refuge, they were back on the job the next day.

These practical words of warning saved the lives of many believers in A.D. 70 when the Roman general Titus came against Jerusalem. They knew that when the Romans desecrated the temple, it was time to head for the hills. They forgot about trying to save valuables and were happy to get out of the city alive. Those in greatest danger were pregnant mothers and those with nursing children (Mark 13:17). Haste was impossible for them. The destruction of Jerusalem is a dark spot in Roman history—not one of Rome's finest hours. They intended to remove the Jewish state from the earth forever.

There is an important lesson to learn from this: Don't expose yourself and your family to unnecessary danger. If you can escape persecution or death without denying your faith or compromising your commitment to Christ, do it. The International Mission Board by policy evacuates Southern Baptist missionaries when their lives are threatened. In spite of this policy some have still paid the supreme price for proclaiming the gospel. Our piety needs to be tempered with common sense in such circumstances. On one occasion Paul left town under the cover of night rather than face an angry crowd the next day (Acts 9:23-25).

your notes

Punchstock

There is also an important encouragement given. "Unless the Lord cut short those days, no one would survive. But because of the elect, whom He chose, He cut short those days" (Mark 13:20). Be encouraged—the Lord controls the duration of tribulation. Be encouraged—the Lord cares for His chosen ones in the tribulation, no matter when and where it takes place.

Tribulation is probably in your future (John 16:33). When it comes, keep your eyes on the Lord and pursue your assignment. Be on your guard lest you fall prey to a false teacher who offers false hope (Mark 13:21-23). Your future is in the hand of a faithful and sovereign God.

Trust God (Mark 13:24-31)

An extended period of suffering can erode one's confidence in God. Exposure to false prophets can compound this problem. It is important that the people of God maintain trust in God in the future. In this section Jesus moved to the climax of all human existence, and it is all about God. Just as the Lord's hand has guided history, He will be in charge in the climax.

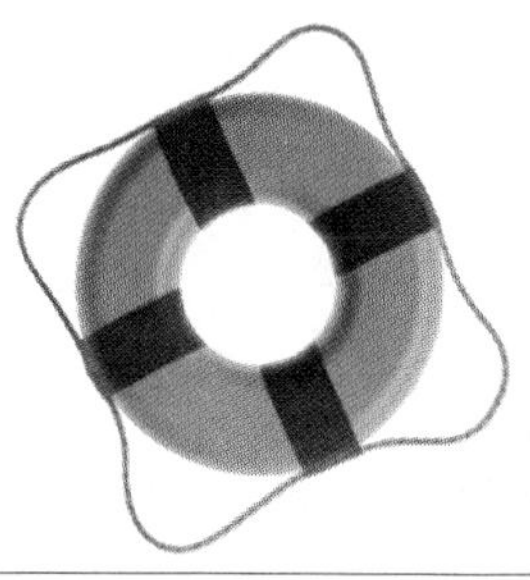

For Your Consideration

1. Some point to fulfilled prophecy as a proof of the unique inspiration of the Bible. Do you agree? Why?

2. Are the words concerning the sun, moon, and stars to be taken literally or symbolically? Why?

3. What is the distinction between the title "Son of Man" and the title "Son of God"?

4. What is the significance of the "clouds" associated with the coming of the Son of Man?

5. If Jesus returns in your lifetime, what do you expect to see?

6. How can we be sure that we are "elect"?

Jesus quoted the ancient prophets—Isaiah and Joel—in describing the climax. These statements come from a context of judgment on the nations and mercy on the people of God. Jesus assured us that God can be trusted; He will stand behind what He has said. The predictions of His prophets will be fulfilled. These statements have a graphic element in them, which may involve symbolic language. Even if the language is symbolic, Jesus' words still speak of an awesome event. God will keep His word. He will judge the human family for their idolatry and their wickedness. Indeed, the whole cosmic order will be involved in this visitation from God. This is a sure word for all of us. Trust God! He will keep His word.

Jesus said that these tribulation events will come to a close when people "see the Son of Man coming in clouds with great power and glory" (v. 26). Here Jesus utilized the words of another prophet—Daniel—in stating the hope of His return. "The Son of Man" is prophetic and messianic language. The title identifies Him with us. He is the exalted and glorified Man. They will see the glorified Man, Jesus, at His triumphal coming. At Jesus' ascension, angels encouraged the disciples, "This Jesus, who has been taken from you into heaven, will come in the same way that you have seen Him going to heaven" (Acts 1:11). Jesus is the Son of God coming as the Son of Man. There will be a personal and visible manifestation of the Son of Man in all His glory.

your notes

Clouds are usually associated with the presence of God, which is the manifestation of the power of God. It will be the luminous clouds that attend the divine presence. What an awesome sight! There will also be the display of His power in judgment on the condemned world. The descriptive words about the cosmic shakeup are the result of the operation of His power. There has never been anything like this in the history of the world. The Sovereign Lord of history is waiting until this climactic moment to give the greatest display of His glory and power in the return of Jesus!

Jesus' coming will not be judgment only. "He will send out the angels and gather His elect from the four winds, from the end of the earth to the end of the sky" (Mark 13:27). This may refer to the rapture (1 Thess. 4:13-17) or to the gathering of Israel for spiritual restoration (Rom. 11:25-27), but in either case it will surely be a display of the faithfulness and the mercy of God as He completes His saving work in His people.

The consummation of the salvation of all the people of God is tied to the coming of Christ (Heb. 9:28). All of His people will be gathered to Him and all will share with Him in the eternal kingdom. This is our blessed hope.

Keep Alert (Mark 13:32-37)

After the parable of the fig tree, which encourages sensitivity to what is happening around us, Jesus ended this look at the future with the admonition, "Be Alert!" (v. 33). This was an appropriate word for the disciples and for His followers in every age, including us.

For Your Consideration

1. Why did Jesus not know the "day" of His return?

2. How should "watching" affect your behavior today?

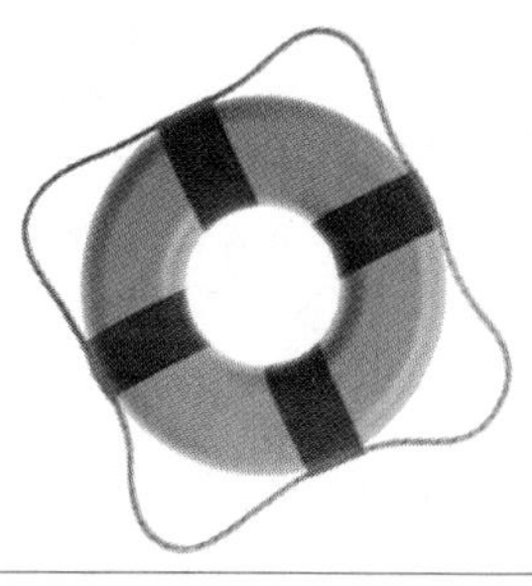

Learning Activity

Personal Assurances

Review Mark 13:9-31 and list the assurances that Jesus gives us about the future. While you are listing each assurance, add a comment about its impact on you personally.

	Assurance	Impact
1.	______________________	______________________
2.	______________________	______________________
3.	______________________	______________________
4.	______________________	______________________
5.	______________________	______________________
6.	______________________	______________________
7.	______________________	______________________

After you finish your list, thank the Lord that we have so many assurances about the future because of Jesus Christ.

your notes

3. Do you agree that the "doorkeeper" may be apostles and pastors? Why or why not?

4. What is your assignment from the Lord?

5. How does the future coming of the Lord affect the way you live your life?

The fact that none of us knows "that day or hour" encourages watchfulness. Because of who Jesus is and who we are, none of us wants to be surprised by His coming. It ought not to bother us that we are left in the dark about that exact moment since even the angels and "the Son" do not know. It would seem that those who set dates for His coming are claiming to know more than Jesus.

Jesus said that He did not know when His return would occur and that only the Father knew (v. 32). This is a reminder to us of the reality of His humanity and the limitations under which He voluntarily lived. He was like us—He had to walk by faith, trusting the faithfulness of the Father.

Watchfulness involves being wide awake and alert. It does not mean that you need to wear special clothing or sit on a hilltop watching the sky as some have done in the past. Rather, it means to live with a readiness to stand before the Lord at a moment's notice.

The parable of the traveling homeowner emphasizes that to watch is to work. Before the homeowner leaves on his long journey, he gives specific assignments to his slaves. He "gave each one his work" (v. 34). He gave the doorkeeper a special charge to stay awake. He gave the assignments, left on his journey, but did not specify the time of his return. The slaves did not know whether it would be "in the evening, or at midnight, or at the crowing of the rooster, or early in the morning" (v. 35). It really does not matter when he returns; they were to have their work done and be ready to receive him.

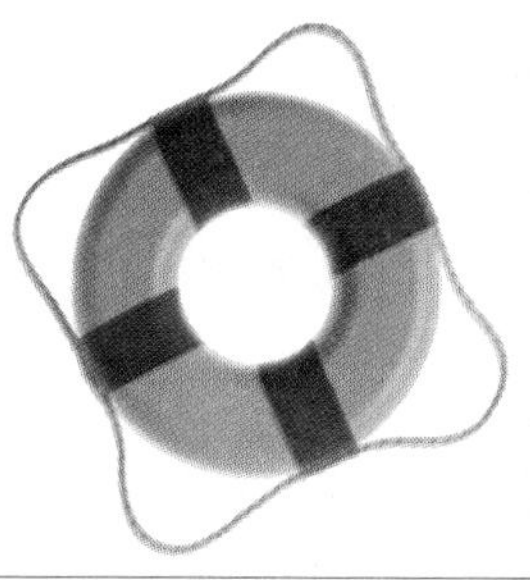

A CLOSER LOOK

Early Christian Martyrs

PERSON	METHOD	YEAR	PLACE
Stephen	Stoned	33	Jerusalem
James	Beheaded	43	Jerusalem
Peter	Crucified	66	Rome
Paul	Beheaded	67	Rome
Ignatius	Burned	115	Rome
Polycarp	Burned	155	Smyrna
Justin	Burned	165	Rome

Jesus is the one taking the long journey. The doorkeeper refers to spiritual leaders like apostles and pastors. We are the slaves under assignment. The best way to demonstrate alertness is by faithfully taking care of your assignment. If the returning Lord finds you doing your job faithfully, His return will be an occasion of great joy!

A stranger asked John Wesley a question about the coming of Christ. He wanted to know what the traveling preacher would do if he knew for sure that Jesus was returning at noon that day. Wesley took his diary from his saddlebag and read out loud his schedule for the rest of the day. Then he said, "That, dear sir, is what I would do." Wesley had it right. You schedule all of life in light of the certainty of our Lord's return and your accountability to Him—even though you do not know the exact time of His coming.

Jesus did not answer all of our questions about the future, but He gave us all of the information we need to guide our plans for the future. The greatest assignment the Lord has given to us is that of making disciples of all the nations. There is much to be done. These words of Jesus about the future should encourage faithfulness in this task.

Session 4

Can I Be Faithful?

Scripture **Mark 14:1–16:8**
Focal: Mark 14:22–42,66–72; 15:33–39; 16:1–8

When I was in college, five young missionaries were martyred in Ecuador. They had attempted to reach out to an isolated tribe of Indians that had never heard the gospel. In their attempt to make contact with the Indians, they landed a small plane near the tribal grounds and waited by a river for the Indians to come to them.

When the Indians came, even though they were hostile, the missionaries made no attempt to flee or to defend themselves. Rather, they died willingly in their effort to demonstrate love and friendship to the Indians. The death of these young men greatly impacted my generation. They had demonstrated what it means to be faithful unto death. Elizabeth Eliot spread the story of their faithfulness as she wrote of her husband Jim's faith in *Through Gates of Splendor*. It forced every Christian who heard about the testimony and faithfulness of these men to ask, "Can I be faithful? What will it cost me?" "Am I willing to make such a sacrifice?"

Mark's Gospel records our Lord's faithfulness to the end—and of the faltering of His disciples. We learn from Him what it means to be faithful. Jesus was faithful to obey His Father in giving His life for our sins, and we can learn from Him what it means to be faithful to obey our Father's will also.

Understand the Ideal (Mark 14:22-31)

The last week in Jesus' life moved at a hectic pace. Every possible moment was spent preparing the disciples for life without His physical presence. Meanwhile, the Jewish leadership plotted His death. There were some uplifting moments such as Jesus' anointing by Mary (vv. 3-9), but there were sobering moments such as the warning about Judas's betrayal (vv. 17-21). But the Passover meal and Jesus' instituting the Lord's Supper were highlights, though the disciples often misunderstood what Jesus said. Jesus told them what was about to happen and how they must remain faithful.

For your consideration

1. What do the wine and bread in the last supper represent?

2. How is the new covenant different from the covenant made at Mount Sinai?

3. Why was Peter so sure he would not fall?

4. What can we learn from Peter's faltering?

The Passover meal was a time of revelation. Jesus interpreted the elements of the Passover meal in a personal way. After saying the prayer of thanksgiving over a loaf of unleavened bread, He broke it and gave it to them to eat and said, "Take [it]; this is My body" (v. 22). Jesus did not mean this literally since He was still physically present. He meant that the bread represented His body and that He wanted them to understand that He is to them spiritually what bread is to them physically. Jesus' death would make this possible.

Then Jesus blessed the cup of wine used in the Passover observance and said, "This is My blood of the covenant, which is shed for many" (v. 24). Covenants in ancient times were often ratified by blood, and Jesus promised the ratification of a new covenant through the shedding of His blood. He referred to the new covenant that God promised through Jeremiah (Jer. 31:31-34), one that was different from the Mosaic covenant. The Passover wine represented His blood that was offered sacrificially at the cross.

your notes

Forgiveness is possible since Jesus faithfully fulfilled His mission as the sacrificial Lamb of God. The new covenant has been ratified and is still in force—in fact, it always will be. We enjoy a totally new relationship with God because of what Jesus accomplished.

While promising to finish His assignment regardless of what it cost, Jesus warned Peter and the others about their vulnerability. Jesus stated, "All of you will fall" (Mark 14:27). He used a prophetic Scripture to warn them that when the shepherd is struck, the sheep will be scattered (see Zech. 13:7).

But Peter would have none of it. He declared, "Even if everyone falls, yet I will not!" (Mark 14:29). When Jesus warned that Peter's fall was imminent—he would deny the Lord three times before the rooster crowed twice to announce another day (v. 30)—Peter continued to insist that he would not fall, as did the others (v. 31). They were all overconfident. They did not realize how threatening an angry crowd could be or how disconcerting it could be for their Shepherd to be arrested and crucified. Presumption is poor preparation for faithfulness.

We must look to Jesus for an example of faithfulness—not His fickle disciples. We must also be careful not to have confidence in our own abilities to remain faithful. Jesus is not only our example of faithfulness but the source of power for our faithfulness.

Pray About God's Will (Mark 14:32-42)

Jesus approached the cross with full awareness of what was happening. This is why He led the disciples to the familiar place of prayer, the garden of Gethsemane. As Jesus went a little farther into the garden with Peter, James, and John, the full force of what He was about to experience overwhelmed Him: "He began to be horrified and deeply distressed" (v. 33). He opened His heart to the three trusted disciples and said,

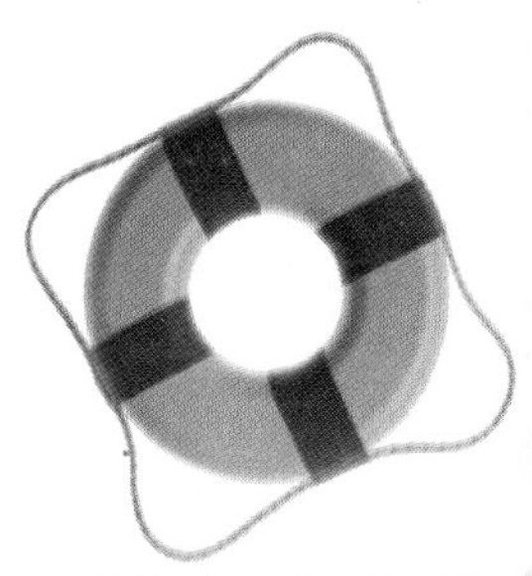

Learning Activity

Perseverance in Prayer

In Mark 14:32-42 Jesus taught some valuable lessons about perseverance in prayer by what He said and did. Learning these lessons can help us persevere as we pray.

Study the following passages, reflect on the questions, and write down your answers.

Read Mark 14:32-34. How will you respond in situations when you are overwhelmed?

Read Mark 14:35-36. How will you handle the tension between what you want and what God wants for you?

Read Mark 14:37-38. How will you deal with those times when you are too tired to pray?

Read Mark 14:39-42. What adjustments will you make in your prayer times (or lack of them) to prepare for the next crisis in your life?

"My soul is swallowed up in sorrow—to the point of death. Remain here and stay awake" (v. 34). The great horror that He faced was the experience of separation from God, becoming the sin offering for the world. What do you do when faithfulness seems to require more than you have to give? Learn from Jesus: pray!

your notes

For Your Consideration

1. Why was Jesus so distressed in the garden?

2. What was in the cup symbolically? What was its significance?

3. How does prayer save us from temptation?

Three times Jesus approached the Father in prayer. The burden of His prayer was that "if it were possible, the hour might pass from Him" (v. 35). The "hour" was the time when He would actually bear the sins of the world as an atoning sacrifice before a holy God. In the prayer He spoke of "this cup." None of us can ever comprehend what it meant for the holy Son of God to bear the penalty of our sins while on the cross. It was unspeakably horrible. But in prayer Jesus surrendered to it, "Abba, Father! All things are possible for You. Take this cup away from Me. Nevertheless, not what I will, but what You will" (v. 36). Jesus surrendered to the will of His Father. (The Aramaic word *Abba* means "father.") Jesus surrendered to His loving and trustworthy Father. He did so with the confidence that the will of His Father was always holy and just.

The humanity of Jesus was real. He shrank from the cross because He knew the ugliness and horror awaiting Him. But the way to faithfulness is to pray the prayer of surrender and move forward in obedience to the will of the Father, regardless of where it may lead.

Jesus strongly admonished a sleepy Peter: "Couldn't you stay awake one hour? Stay awake and pray, so that

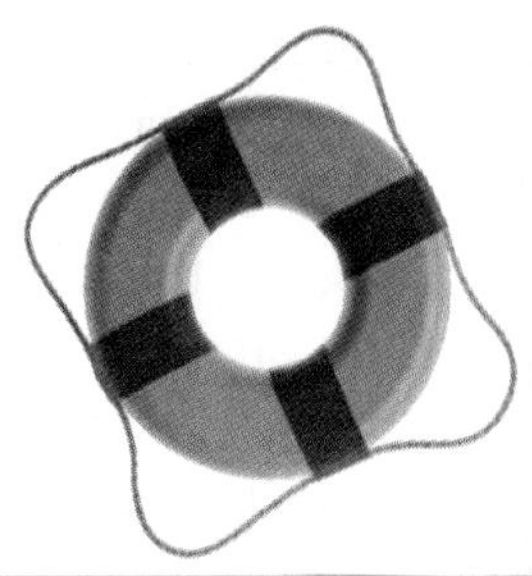

you won't enter into temptation. The spirit is willing, but the flesh is weak" (vv. 37-38). The inner confidence of the disciples would soon be shattered. They thought they were ready for whatever might happen. They did not feel the need to pray. They did not realize the weakness of their flesh. "Flesh" was often used for the physical body, but it normally refers to the frailty and weaknesses of human nature (Rom. 7:18,25). The strength needed to be faithful comes as we seek the Father in prayer. We cannot find it in ourselves.

You are not ready for the tests of life when you sleep through prayer time. Strength comes through prayer. Jesus left the garden full of the strength needed for faithfulness, but the disciples left vulnerable to temptation.

Repent for Failure (Mark 14:66-72)

The contrast between Jesus and His chief apostle is dramatic. Peter failed terribly. Even though he did follow Jesus at a distance (v. 54) while the others ran, he shamefully denied the Lord three times.

For your consideration

1. What is the difference between Peter's denial of Jesus and Judas's betrayal of Jesus?

2. What kind of oath did Peter take in the denial?

3. How might a modern disciple deny Jesus?

4. Why was Peter so devastated by the crowing of the rooster?

Love and loyalty demanded more of Peter than he had the strength to give. He was in another section of the high priest's quarters when the first denial occurred (v. 66). A servant of the high priest recognized him and blurted out, "You also were with that Nazarene, Jesus" (v. 67). Peter's denial was immediate. A little later she pressed the case, and Peter denied his relationship with Jesus a second time (vv. 69-70). A while later it happened the third time. This time he was even bolder in his denial: "Then he started to curse and to swear with an oath" (vv. 70-71). This is more serious than using some curse words—he actually used the name of God in taking an oath affirming that he had no acquaintance with Jesus. Even

your notes

though he had been with Jesus for three years and knew in his heart that Jesus was the Messiah, he denied Him.

Peter was thinking only of himself at this point. The fear in Peter was stronger than his desire to please the Lord. The lesson is that if Peter can deny the Lord, surely we are all vulnerable to that possibility.

The rooster played a prominent part in this incident. A rooster crowed right after his first denial, but it was the second crowing of the rooster that got his attention (v. 68,72). Just after his third and most emphatic denial of the Lord, he heard the rooster. Then he remembered. He recalled the warning that Jesus had given him. "When he thought about it, he began to weep" (v. 72). Peter's tears were an expression of genuine sorrow over his failure. Repentance involves more than sorrow over your failure, but sorrow is the first step toward repentance. The sorrow prepared Peter for the restoration that would take place after Jesus' resurrection.

Do you have a painful memory of unfaithfulness? Peter is a reminder that your failure does not have to be final. His most fruitful days of service and most faithful witness to Jesus came after his shameful failure. There is hope for all of us who have failed Jesus at times.

Be Willing to Suffer (Mark 15:33-39)

Mark's account of the crucifixion of Jesus was confined to the essentials. He made no attempt to appeal to our emotions; rather, he just stated the facts about the event. It followed a night of trial before the Jewish court and the high priest (14:53-65). They convicted Jesus of blasphemy and decided He should die. Since they could not impose the death penalty, they led Him away to stand before Pilate, the Roman governor (15:1)

After examining Him, Pilate found Jesus innocent of any capital crime and tried to release Him (vv. 2-14). Pilate finally gave in to the pressure of the crowd led by the Jewish leaders and condemned Jesus to die by

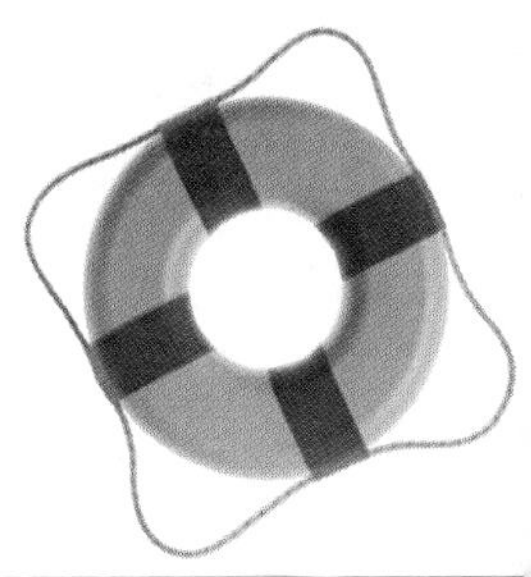

Learning Activity

Perseverance and Faithfulness

Mark 14:1–16:8 underscores the importance of persevering as we serve the Lord. Reflect on the lessons you have learned about perseverance and . . .

partaking in the Lord's Supper (Mark 14:22-25)

praying (Mark 14:32-42)

repenting (Mark 14:66-72)

suffering (Mark 15:33-39)

Jesus' resurrection (Mark 16:1-8)

Turn these lessons into commitments to grow stronger in your faithfulness to Christ. What will you do with what you have learned?

your notes

crucifixion (vv. 15-26). While some mocked and others just watched, Jesus was nailed to the cross between two criminals. This happened about 9:00 a.m.—the third hour by Roman reckoning of time.

For your consideration

1. What was the significance of the three hours of darkness?

2. What did it mean for Jesus to experience being forsaken of God?

3. Why was the curtain in the temple torn when Jesus died?

4. What in the death of Jesus convinced the centurion that He was the Son of God?

The darkness that came on the land at noon was a sign of the judgment of God falling on sin. Jesus had taken on Himself the sins of the world, and the darkness expressed visually what it means to be separated from God. It was the hour of judgment for human sin when Jesus became the sacrifice for our sins.

Jesus endured the darkness for three hours, and then He cried out, "My God, My God, why have You forsaken me?" (v. 34), a quotation of Psalm 22:1. How are we to understand these words? Do they express what Jesus was actually experiencing, or do they express Jesus' confidence in God in a terrible situation? Probably both. On the cross Jesus experienced separation from God, which is the divine penalty for sin. But Jesus was also confident that this separation would not be permanent.

If we are to be faithful, we have to follow Jesus' example. No believer will ever experience the pain that Jesus endured, but we may have to suffer even though we don't understand the reason for it.

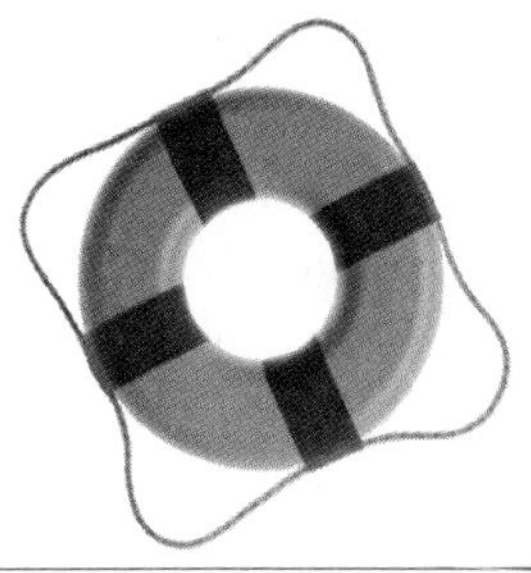

Jesus' death is remarkable. Most people died from exhaustion and weakness when crucified, but Jesus still had strength enough for a loud cry when He "breathed His last" (Mark 15:37). He was faithful even unto death. His obedience to the Father was complete.

The Father gave an immediate indication of the completeness of His obedience when He caused the curtain in the sanctuary to "split in two from top to bottom" (v. 38). The sacrifice of the Son rendered the old system of the temple useless. Jesus' death marked a new beginning in the relationship between God and man. The confession of the centurion is a foretaste of what is to come. This Roman soldier confessed, "This man really was God's Son!" (v. 39). He may have confessed more than he understood, but it was nothing less than the truth.

We should be prepared to be faithful even unto death. The Father who gave His Son for us deserves no less. The Son who gave Himself for us deserves it.

Be Certain of Triumph (Mark 16:1-8)

Joseph of Arimathea, "a prominent member of the Sanhedrin who was himself looking forward to the kingdom of God" (15:43), laid Jesus to rest. Some faithful women watched the whole procedure (v. 47). This was accomplished just as the Sabbath approached on Friday evening. It appeared that the faithfulness of Jesus had accomplished nothing.

For Your Consideration

1. Why did none of the disciples expect the resurrection of Jesus?

2. Why was Peter singled out in the commission to the women?

3. Why is the resurrection of Jesus so important to the Christian faith?

The Sabbath was a day of mourning and despair. It was over. Jesus was dead. It had happened so suddenly. The disciples must have felt shame over their failures on Thursday night and Friday. Surely Jesus had deserved more loyalty than He had received from them.

Dawn on Sunday found some of the faithful women on their way to the tomb. They took with them spices to anoint the body. They intended to make sure the body of Jesus had been properly anointed for burial. Their

your notes

discussion, as they went toward the tomb, centered on how they would gain entrance to the tomb. They knew they would not be able to roll the stone away (vv. 1-3). What they found caught them totally by surprise.

They arrived at the tomb and noticed that the large stone that covered the entrance had been rolled away. After they cautiously entered the tomb, they noticed immediately that the body was gone. Instead of Jesus' body, they saw a "young man dressed in a long white robe sitting on the right side" (vv. 4-5). Matthew identified the young man as an angel (Matt. 28:2-7). The women "were amazed and alarmed" (Mark 16:5). They were gripped by a mixture of fear and utter despair.

The angel had good news for the women. They had no reason to be alarmed. "You are looking for Jesus the Nazarene, who was crucified. He has been resurrected! He is not here! See the place where they put Him" (v. 6).

The women were given an assignment: "But go, tell His disciples and Peter" (v. 7). Only Mark included this word about Peter, which is especially meaningful if this Gospel is based on Peter's memories (as early church history contends). Though the disciples ran from Jesus in fear on Thursday and Peter denied Him three times, He still claimed them as His disciples. He would meet with them in Galilee and renew their commission. But the women were so overwhelmed with what they had heard that they ran from the tomb trembling and kept the whole thing to themselves (v. 8).

Many scholars consider verses 9-20 a later addition to the Gospel since they do not occur in many older manuscripts. Therefore it seems likely that Mark ended his Gospel with the angel's pronouncement of Jesus' resurrection. The tomb is empty and the crucified One lives. The resurrection of Jesus assures believers of eternal life and proves that God rewards faithfulness. When we are tempted to abandon our assignment, we must remember that faithfulness leads to triumph. Jesus' resurrection turned great tragedy into victory.

A CLOSER LOOK

Crucifixion: A Common Death

Various forms of crucifixion were practiced in ancient times, but the Romans modified it for their purposes and used it extensively. Initially, only slaves could be crucified, but eventually so could Roman citizens if so decreed by Caesar. Victims were flogged beforehand as punishment and to hasten death, and then they were forced to carry the crossbeam to the execution site where the vertical crosspiece was already in place. Victims were either tied or nailed to the cross; nails were used if a quicker death were desired—as in Jesus' case since the Sabbath was approaching. Victims often survived for several days, an especially powerful deterrent for observers. Crosses were of four shapes: the 't'; the 'T'; the 'X'; and the '+'. A placard engraved with the legal charge for which a victim was being executed was placed either around the neck or above the victim's head; the latter was the case for Jesus (see Matt. 27:37; John 19:19), indicating that the traditional 't' shape for His cross is likely correct. Sometimes the Jews practiced crucifixion. In 76 B.C. the priest-king Alexander Janneus had eight hundred Pharisees crucified for revolt. But the Romans were the champions: Caesar Augustus boasted that he had crucified all unclaimed slaves from thirty thousand captured; and in response to the Spartacus-led slave revolt (71 B.C.), the Romans lined both sides of the Appian Way (a 132-mile road) with six thousand crucified.

CHRISTIAN GROWTH STUDY PLAN

In the **Christian Growth Study Plan (formerly Church Study Course),** this book *Hope When Believers Struggle: Studies in Mark's Gospel* is a resource for course credit in one Leadership and Skill Development diploma and two Christian Growth diploma plans. To receive credit, read the book, complete the learning activities, show your work to your pastor, a staff member or church leader, then complete the information on the next page. The form may be duplicated. Send the completed page to:

Christian Growth Study Plan
One LifeWay Plaza
Nashville, TN 37234-0117
FAX: (615)251-5067
Email: cgspnet@lifeway.com

For information about the Christian Growth Study Plan, refer to the Christian Growth Study Plan Catalog. It is located online at www.lifeway.com/cgsp. If you do not have access to the Internet, contact the Christian Growth Study Plan office (1.800.968.5519) for the specific plan you need for your ministry.

Hope When Believers Struggle: Studies in Mark's Gospel

❑ CG-1041 ❑ LS-5053 (Sunday School)

PARTICIPANT INFORMATION

Social Security Number (USA ONLY-optional)	Personal CGSP Number*	Date of Birth (MONTH, DAY, YEAR)
Name (First, Middle, Last)		Home Phone
Address (Street, Route, or P.O. Box)	City, State, or Province	Zip/Postal Code

Please check appropriate box: ❑ Resource purchased by self ❑ Resource purchased by church ❑ Other

CHURCH INFORMATION

Church Name		
Address (Street, Route, or P.O. Box)	City, State, or Province	Zip/Postal Code

CHANGE REQUEST ONLY

☐ Former Name		
☐ Former Address	City, State, or Province	Zip/Postal Code
☐ Former Church	City, State, or Province	Zip/Postal Code

Signature of Pastor, Conference Leader, or Other Church Leader	Date

*New participants are requested but not required to give SS# and date of birth. Existing participants, please give CGSP# when using SS# for the first time. Thereafter, only one ID# is required. **Mail to:** Christian Growth Study Plan, One LifeWay Plaza, Nashville, TN 37234-0117. Fax: (615)251-5067.

Rev. 3-03